Irish Quaker Hybrid Identities

Quaker Studies

Volumes published in this Brill Research Perspectives title are listed at brill.com/*rpqs*

Irish Quaker Hybrid Identities

Complex Identity in the Religious Society of Friends

By

Maria H. Kennedy

BRILL

LEIDEN | BOSTON

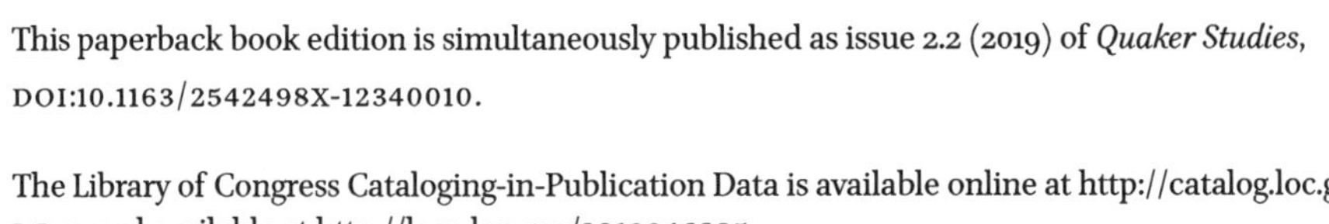

This paperback book edition is simultaneously published as issue 2.2 (2019) of *Quaker Studies*, DOI:10.1163/2542498X-12340010.

The Library of Congress Cataloging-in-Publication Data is available online at http://catalog.loc.gov
LC record available at http://lccn.loc.gov/2019946235

Typeface for the Latin, Greek, and Cyrillic scripts: "Brill". See and download: brill.com/brill-typeface.

ISBN 978-90-04-41518-8 (paperback)
ISBN 978-90-04-41519-5 (e-book)

This book is printed on acid-free paper and produced in a sustainable manner.

Printed by Printforce, the Netherlands

To my grandchildren
Shantaya and Jonah

∵

Contents

Irish Quaker Identities: Complex Identity in the Religious Society of Friends

Maria Kennedy
Independent scholar, Bristol, UK
mariahkennedy@hotmail.com

Abstract

This work is a sociological study of Quakers, which investigates the impact that sectarianism has had on identity construction within the Religious Society of Friends in Ireland. The research highlights individual Friends' complex and hybrid cultural, national and theological identities, mirrored by the Society's corporate identity. This publication focuses specifically on examples of political and theological hybridity. These hybrid identities resulted in tensions that impact on relationships between Friends and the wider organisation. How Friends negotiate and accommodate these diverse identities is explored. It is argued that Irish Quakers prioritise 'relational unity' and have developed a distinctive approach to complex identity management. It is asserted that in the two Irish states, 'Quaker' represents a meta-identity, which is counter-cultural in its non-sectarianism, although this is more problematic within the organisation. Furthermore, by modelling an alternative, non-sectarian identity, Quakers in Ireland contribute to building capacity for transformation from oppositional, binary identities to more fluid and inclusive ones.

Keywords

Quakers – Ireland – sectarianism – identity – hybrid – unity

 | DOI:10.1163/9789004415195_002

1 Introduction

In this publication I argue that sectarianism in Ireland has had a distinctive impact on the identity of Irish Quakers.[1] The resulting diverse and complex identity of Ireland Yearly Meeting (IYM) has caused tensions between Friends arising from their hybrid political and theological identities. Consequently, in order to maintain the unity of the organisation, Ireland Yearly Meeting has developed an approach to identity management which prioritises relationships between Friends.

These findings are based on fieldwork carried out in 2011 and 2012, using in-depth semi-structured interviews and one follow up interview in 2019. Participants in this study were identified through contacts that put me in touch with Irish Friends, networking at Quaker events, letters to the clerks of Preparative Meetings (PMs) and a notice about my research in the Irish Quaker magazine *The Friendly Word.* A total of 15 people agreed to be interviewed, and they came from Meetings both in the Republic of Ireland and Northern Ireland. I also corresponded with a number of other Irish Friends who provided useful background information about the culture of Irish Quakerism. In addition, there were two British Quakers who had been based at Quaker House in Belfast, who agreed to be interviewed about their impressions of IYM.

In this section I outline the main arguments underpinning the publication, with a particular focus on how the legacy of sectarianism in Ireland has impacted on the identity of Friends there. I provide an introduction to the establishment of the Quaker movement in England and then an outline of the theology and culture of Irish Quakerism. I provide a summary of the origins of sectarianism and discuss my approach to the complex issue of language, terminology and historical 'balance' to fairly represent the narratives and perspectives of the two main political/religious traditions in Ireland. I then go on to introduce some of the main themes related to the case study of Irish Quaker identity, identity theory and sectarianism.

Section 2 begins with a brief introduction to Quakerism in Ireland, the nature of sectarianism in the Irish context and the impact on the positioning and culture of the Society. In section 3 there is a review of the main theoretical perspectives about identity with a particular focus on oppositional identity in Ireland. Section 4 explores the hybrid political and theological identity of Irish Friends through two case studies. Section 5 looks at the management of these

1 Friend and Quaker are used interchangeably throughout the publication.

diverse identities by Ireland Yearly Meeting and section 6 draws together these different themes and my conclusions.

1.1 *Background to the Establishment of Quakerism*

The Religious Society of Friends emerged in England in the period following the English civil war. John Punshon states that they were one of the many radical Protestant nonconformist groups who believed that the Reformation did not go far enough in breaking with the religious practises and structures of Catholicism (1984, 9–10). Gerard Guiton outlines the social upheaval of the times in the aftermath of the war and widespread reaction against injustices inherent in English society such as rent increases and payment of tithes.[2] According to Guiton, Quakerism emerged with the intention of bringing people the 'light' of spiritual solace (2005, 5). Furthermore, Guiton states that the centrality of theological concerns at the time were to do with growing dissatisfaction with the lingering influence of Catholicism on the Established Church (2005, 6).

Punshon dates the establishment of Quakerism as a religious group from 1652 when George Fox[3] felt called by God to climb Pendle Hill in Lancashire and had a vision of a 'gathered people'. Fox travelled further north and began preaching his message rejecting traditional forms of worship and teaching that people should listen to the 'inner light' of Christ's guidance (1984, 53–54). Fox attracted many who were 'convinced'[4] by his teachings and also much opposition because of his criticism of traditional church services, structures and authority (Punshon 1984, 57). In the early period of Quakerism evangelists went on to take their message to other countries including Ireland, the Netherlands, Germany and some of the American colonies (Punshon 1984, 69).

Pink Dandelion and Peter Collins assert that 'Quakers were the most successful sect of republican rule' and that Quakerism can be viewed as radical in

2 Tithes were mandatory payments to local clergy and were a major source of discontent during the civil war period when many people stopped paying them. According to Barry Reay, Quakers were at the forefront of anti-tithing agitation and were particularly associated with this campaign (1980, 98–99).

3 George Fox (1624–1691) was the main founder of Quakerism (Dandelion 2008b, 2). He was one of a number of radical Christians in England who believed they were part of a movement to restore the 'True Church'.

4 Guiton states that 'convincement' was a form of spiritual baptism and opening up to God. Friends were expected to share their experience of being 'convinced' with others in their Meetings to deepen the spiritual growth of the community (2005, 47). The current use of the term refers to adults who become members of the Society 'by convincement' (Dandelion 2008b, 130).

the sense that early Friends believed that everyone can have a direct spiritual experience with the Divine that does not have to be mediated by another and that this could be achieved more effectively in a Meeting for Worship based on silence. Quakers also believed in the equality of all so that everyone could 'minister'[5] if called to do so (Dandelion and Collins 2008, 2).

The Manchester Conference of Quakers in 1895 is generally acknowledged as marking the decline of evangelical Quakerism in Britain Yearly Meeting (BYM) and the ascendency of liberal Quakerism (Cantor 2001, 322). According to Dandelion and Collins:

> … by 1900, Quakerism had been re-visioned by its younger adherents as part of liberal Christianity. It was also redesigned as again distinctively Quaker: Experience was primary. Liberal Friends did not want to return to the earlier days and they envisioned a Quakerism relevant to the age, open to new ideas, and one which held to the idea of progressive revelation, that God necessarily revealed more over time. (2008, 3)

Dandelion outlines the different theological perspectives of liberal and evangelical Friends about the role of the scriptures and the 'inner light' (1996, 10). Liberal Friends were strongly influenced by Darwinism[6] and turned to the ideas of early Quakers, re-establishing the notion of the 'inner light' and focus on individual discernment[7] and experience. The Bible, although a source of inspiration, was not held to have authority by liberal Friends, unlike evangelical Quakers (Dandelion 1996, 12).

In contemporary times Friends refer to the testimonies of truth and integrity; justice, equality and community; simplicity and peace, and more recently earth and the environment as guidance for how to put their faith into action (Quakers in Britain). In discussing the historic association of Quakers with the peace testimony, Dandelion adds that:

---

5 Ministry is the personal testimony of Friends' experience of connection with God or 'the light' (Dandelion 1996, 16).

6 One of the speakers at the Manchester Conference was the physicist Silvanus Phillips. According to Geoffrey Cantor, 'he argued that modern science had brought new and valuable insights into the world, for example, the theory of evolution, that contemporary Quakers must fully engage [with]' (2001, 336).

7 'Discernment: The process by which Quakers decide what is truly from God' (Dandelion 2008b, 130).

> Within the liberal tradition, the emphasis on experience allowed those with less-defined faith or clearly non-Christian ideas, but drawn by this testimony, to find a place within Quakerism. (2008a, 67)

1.2 *Quakers in Ireland – Theology and Culture*

Elizabeth Duke identifies four main strands of worldwide Quakerism today; they are: Evangelical, Orthodox, Conservative and Liberal. Ireland Yearly Meeting (IYM)[8] has a unique position in world Quakerism because it includes both evangelical and liberal Quakers and is unprogrammed, meaning that Meetings for Worship follow the pattern of silence with ministry (Duke 2012a, 6).

The testimonies have particular significance for Quakers in Ireland. Throughout the publication I give examples of how different interpretations of the testimonies of peace, truth and equality, in particular, caused contention within IYM. Dandelion's assertion that contemporary British Quakerism is post-Christian (2008a, 22) is less applicable in the context of IYM. Many respondents observed that the culture of Irish Quakerism, even among liberal Friends, remains more Christo-centric than that of Britain Yearly Meeting, reflecting the continuing significance of religion in the two Irish states.[9]

I explore this theme with reference to the table developed by Dandelion outlining the different perspectives of Evangelical, Conservative and Liberal Friends (2008b, 108–109). In the amended Table 1.1 (Dandelion 2008b, 108–109) the details about Conservative theology have been removed and I have added a column comparing the general perspectives of liberal and evangelical Quakers with those of Quakers in Ireland.

8 Ireland Yearly Meeting is the name of both the national organisation of Quakers in Ireland and the annual gathering of Friends.

9 Although, as Gladys Ganiel contends, research studies point to the Catholic Church no longer being such a dominating force in Irish society leading to some commentators referring to Ireland as being post-Catholic. This development is linked to concerns about clerical abuse, criticism of the Catholic educational system in the Republic of Ireland and the impact of increasing immigration leading to greater religious and ethnic diversity in the two Irish states (2016, 294–295). There is also an increasing trend towards secularisation which has impacted on other Christian denominations (personal correspondence, 2019).

TABLE 1 Areas of difference between evangelical, conservative and liberal friends

Evangelical	Liberal	Irish Quaker
Scripture and spiritual experience as primary	Experience as primary	Scripture and experience equally primary
Defined by belief	Defined in terms of method/form	Defined by belief and form
Christian identity primary	'Quaker' identity primary	Christian and 'Quaker' identity equally primary
Christian	Christian, post-Christian, and non-theist	Christian and non-theist
Realism	Semi-realism and non-realism	Realism and semi-realism
Final and complete and whole Truth possible. Theology as True, not just story.	Truth only personal, partial, or provisional. Theology always a 'towards' kind of activity. The 'absolute perhaps'.	Final and complete and whole Truth possible. Theology as True, not just story. Truth only personal, partial, or provisional.
Programmed or semi-programmed worship	Unprogrammed worship	Unprogrammed worship and semi-programmed worship
Pastors – visible and active	No visible leadership	Leadership role taken on by 'weighty' Friends to manage complex identity
Restraint of emotion variable church by church	Restraint of emotion	Restraint of emotion variable Meeting by Meeting
Mission Christianity seen as salvific	Outreach Quakerism seen as optional	Limited outreach
Traditional teaching on sexual morality	Politically liberal on sexual morality	Mix of traditional and liberal teaching on sexual morality
Inclusive	Exclusive?	Inclusive? – complicated by spectrum of theological outlook

The differences between the strands of Quakerism in the first two columns in Table 1 and Irish Quaker theology reflect the spectrum of belief within IYM, different forms of worship, leadership roles and the identities of Friends. For example, there are different teachings about sexual morality that have to be accommodated within IYM. The outward form of Irish Quakerism is primarily liberal in the sense that worship is generally unprogrammed and there are no pastors. A number of these themes will be developed more fully in the publication.

According to a respondent who shared their impressions of Quaker identity in Ireland, the 'Troubles'[10] brought some changes in the culture of Irish Quakerism. I was told that although not many people joined the Religious Society of Friends during this period; the new ones tended to be drawn to the peace testimony and also that those people were quite active. Apparently this was very different from the culture of the old established Quaker families, who were predominantly 'birthright' Friends. This respondent asserted that newer Friends were disaffected by their previous Churches (for example, those from Roman Catholic and Church of Ireland backgrounds) for theological and structural reasons, and were looking for the new more open structure that they found in Quakerism. Thus identity became different – rather than one clear Quaker identity there were three or four different identities that were equally strong and consequently there was a greater need for tolerance of each other. There was a sense that Friends from different traditions co-existed rather than really accepting each other (personal correspondence, 2012). Ross Chapman identifies this change as being linked to adherents from a culturally-Catholic background who joined the Society in the 1970s (2013, 16). Additionally, a number of respondents have commented on the distinctive regional subcultures in IYM.

10 According to Melaugh and Lynn (2005), the term the 'Troubles' is a euphemism used by people in Ireland for the most recent conflict and it has been used before to describe other periods of Irish history. An example of the previous use of the term is given by O'Connor in his book *The Troubles: the Struggle for Irish Freedom 1912–1922*, which describes the period leading up to the partition of Ireland (1989). The current use of the expression refers to violent conflict in Ireland between 1968 and 1998. The violence mainly impacted on people living in Northern Ireland but also resulted in casualties in the Republic and mainland Britain. According to Clem McCartney (1999, 17), at the height of the 'Troubles' in 1972 a total of 467 people were killed including 321 civilians. Different statistics are quoted by other commentators for that year, for example, 497 deaths including 259 civilians (McKittrick and McVea 2001, 325). This discrepancy is likely to reflect the difficulty in accurately categorising 'Troubles'-related deaths and injuries.

1.3 *Sectarianism in Ireland*

Sectarian divisions on the island of Ireland have been shaped by historical, social and theological factors which have had a profound impact on identity. Joseph Liechty and Cecelia Clegg define sectarianism in the Irish context as:

> a system of attitudes, actions, beliefs and structures at personal, communal, and institutional levels which always involves religion, and typically involves a negative mixing of religion and politics which arises as a distorted expression of positive, human needs especially for belonging, identity and the free expression of difference and is expressed in destructive patterns of relating.... (2001, 102–103)

The roots of sectarianism can be traced to the colonial period in Ireland which began with the Anglo-Norman conquest of the country in 1169. According to Tim Pat Coogan,[11] for nationalists in Ireland this event marks the beginning of 'eight hundred years of British oppression' (1995, 3). During the next four centuries attempts were made by successive English monarchs to extend control over the rest of Ireland. By the end of the Elizabethan period much of the country had been conquered with the exception of Ulster which was more difficult to subdue (Coohill 2008, 20).

A key period in terms of the consolidation of English rule and sectarian division dates from 1609 and is known as the 'Plantation of Ulster' (Darby 1995, 3). Anglican and Presbyterian colonists from England and Scotland were encouraged to settle in Ulster and were given large tracts of land. In return they were required to bring Protestant tenants as farm workers (Coohill 2008, 21). The new landowners introduced their own form of agriculture and settlements and Joseph Coohill argues that these changes drove a further wedge between the native Irish and the newcomers (2008, 21–22). According to Nicholas Frayling, many of them were forced off their land into destitution and starvation. Economic and social divisions between the native Irish and new settlers were compounded by the religious divide and the negative stereotypes of the Irish prevalent in English society at the time (1996, 141).

---

11 Tim Pat Coogan has a background in journalism and writes about Irish history from a distinctively nationalist perspective. I have included references to Coogan's work, despite the potential bias inherent in this source, because they illustrate an important strand of thinking in popular discourse about the link between sectarianism and colonialism in Ireland.

Liechty and Clegg argue that these divisions were also reinforced by the powerful position of the Church of Ireland which was the Established Church until 1870 (2001, 71). Marianne Elliott suggests that by the eighteenth century the penal laws established the link between political loyalty and the Established Church with the exclusion of Catholics and Dissenters from public office and certain professions. The outcome was that the Church of Ireland and its members were privileged in Irish society (2009, 96). Elliot argues that although the term 'Protestant ascendancy' is generally understood to mean 'the monopoly of propertied Protestants of Irish political life in the eighteenth century'. It was also seen at the time as representing the dominant position of all Protestants in Irish society not just the elite (2009, 111).

Another significant event in terms of the entrenchment of political sectarianism was the 1798 Rebellion. This was a failed attempt by Catholic and Protestant nationalists, known as the 'United Irishmen', under the leadership of the Protestant reformer, Theobald Wolfe Tone, to stage an armed insurrection against British colonial rule in Ireland with the support of French naval forces (Coohill 2008, 32). Mitchell suggests that the participation of Presbyterians in this event was a rare example of the involvement of Dissenters in a nationalist cause, suggesting that 'historically, the dominant trend has been for Protestant Churches to rally behind the unionist political mainstream' (2006, 48). However, Peter Berresford Ellis argues that at this point Nationalism was still a political force rather than exclusively associated with Catholicism (2004, 6). The British government responded to the Rebellion by passing an Act of Union in 1801 bringing Ireland under direct rule from Westminster and the Irish parliament which met in Dublin was abolished (Darby 1995, 4).

Berresford Ellis suggests that in the period after 1798 most of the penal laws against Dissenters were removed to shore up support for English colonial rule in Ireland (2004, 6). However, the requirement to pay tithes only ended with the disestablishment of the Church of Ireland (Smith 2001, 560). During the time of what became known as the 'Great Famine' 1845–52,[12] the British government and what Ó hEithir describes as 'proselytising Protestants' (1989, 41) set up relief schemes in return for work.[13] Coohill states that there is a broad consensus that over a million people died of starvation and disease and that

12 In 1845 blight destroyed most of the potato harvest in the south-east of the country. By 1847 the blight had spread throughout Ireland and almost the whole crop was destroyed (Frayling 1996, 146).

13 However, there were exceptions to this approach. Quakers in Ireland had a reputation for providing unconditional relief during the 'Great Famine' (Coohill 2008, 67).

more than a million emigrated in order to escape the crisis (2008, 59). Frayling adds that the population had halved by the end of the 1800s (1996, 147).

Coohill argues that the political impact of the famine was profound and far reaching. Some Irish people who emigrated to North America and Australia during this time connected with Republican networks which raised funds and provided weapons for future Republican insurrections in Ireland. Coohill asserts that the British government's response to the famine also added to the bitter folk memories about colonial rule in Ireland (2008, 72–73). Roy Foster refers to this as '… the export of a race-memory of horror' (1992, 167). Coohill suggests that the famine also had a negative impact on relationships between Catholics and Protestants in Ireland; it was regarded by both communities as mainly affecting Catholics, who saw themselves as victims of British policy, and those Protestants who felt they were spared by divine providence because they were not Catholic (2008, 74). The differential impact of the famine resulted in an increase in sectarian divisions between the communities in Belfast and other areas of the north-east, where a number of Catholics and Protestants had moved to escape death and disease during the famine years (Coohill 2008, 74).

In the 1870s Irish nationalists campaigned vigorously for a restoration of Home Rule for Ireland. In the British parliament the prime minister, W.E. Gladstone, attempted on two occasions to introduce a Home Rule Bill in order to resolve the 'Irish question'. On the third attempt in 1912, Gladstone was successful but due to the outbreak of the First World War, the passage of the bill into law was deferred (McKittrick and McVea 2001, 3). Ulster unionists were angry about the possibility of loosening their ties with Britain and regarded the Home Rule campaign as a way of establishing a Catholic ascendancy in Ireland (Elliott 2009, 140). The Unionist leader, Edward Carson, formed a militia called the 'Ulster Volunteer Force' in 1913 to defend Ulster if Home Rule was implemented. According to Berresford Ellis the campaign slogan, 'Home Rule is Rome Rule', demonstrated the sectarian nature of the anti-Home Rule campaign (2004, 205).

Although movements such as the Home Rule campaign sought independence by parliamentary means, other organisations such as the Irish Republican Brotherhood (IRB) were committed to the use of armed force (Darby 1995, 4). The IRB staged an armed insurrection in Dublin in 1916 which came to be known as 'the Easter Rising'.[14] The Easter Rising led to unionist

14 The event known as the Easter Rising (because it started on Easter Monday 1916) was an armed insurrection against British rule organised by the Supreme Council of the Irish Republican Brotherhood, a military organisation with strong links to Irish-American republicans (O'Connor 1989, 71). Republicans took over the General Post Office in Dublin

accusations that nationalists had taken advantage of Britain being at war to stage this insurrection, asserting that those involved in the Rising were traitors (Coohill 2008, 126). However, according to Coohill, the reaction of the British authorities in executing fifteen of the leaders of the Rising and imprisoning many more in English jails created more Irish martyrs and increased support for the Republican cause (2008, 127). Despite the failure of the Rising at the time, its commemoration subsequently became a seminal event in the Republican movement north and south of the border and a trigger point for sectarian violence, especially during the 'Troubles' (Wood 2009, 20).

In 1919 the nationalist party in Ireland, Sinn Féin (SF), set up a parliament in Dublin called the Dáil Éireann and declared an all-Ireland Republic. The Irish Republican Army (IRA) began a series of attacks on the Royal Irish Constabulary (RIC) which triggered the Anglo-Irish war 1919–21 (Coohill 2008, 128). The British government had recognised that the imposition of Home Rule for the whole of Ireland on Ulster unionists would be very difficult to enforce and passed the Government of Ireland Act (1920). This legislation set out the intention to create two Irish states: the Irish Free State and the Province of Northern Ireland. There were to be two parliaments, one in Dublin and the other in Belfast. Each parliament was to have a measure of self-government.[15] Although unionists in the north accepted the legislation, republicans in Ireland decided that they no longer wanted Home Rule but an independent Republic and the hostilities between the IRA and British forces continued (McKittrick and McVea 2001, 4).

A delegation of Irish representatives led by Michael Collins (Minister of Finance in the Dáil Éireann) came to London in 1921 to discuss a peace agreement. According to Coohill, with the threat of all-out war by Lloyd George the Irish delegation reluctantly signed the Anglo-Irish Treaty which gave the Free State dominion or self-governing status within the British Commonwealth and set up a boundary commission to work out how the country was to be partitioned (2008, 129–130). The partition of Ireland eventually left twenty-six counties in the Irish Free State and the remaining six counties in the Province

where one of the leaders, Padraig Pearse, read out a Declaration from 'the Provisional Government of the Irish Republic' to the people of Ireland (O'Connor 1989, 81). According to Ulick O'Connor, the Rising was very badly organised, the leaders had conflicting views and strategies and the arms due to arrive from Germany were never delivered due to miscommunication (1989, 79).

15 Kenneth Bloomfield adds that the Government of Ireland Act provided for two parliaments but also included provision for a Council of Ireland that eventually envisioned one parliament for the whole of Ireland; partition was not regarded as a permanent 'solution' at the time (2007, 6).

of Northern Ireland which functioned as a self-governing region of the United Kingdom (Berresford Ellis 2004, 7).[16]

1.4 *The Irish Free State*

The early years of the new Free State were dominated by conflict between republicans about the Anglo-Irish Treaty that had partitioned Ireland and the legitimacy of the Dáil Éireann for its role in ratifying the Treaty. Irish republicans were split between those for and against the Treaty and a civil war broke out in 1922. Ultimately the Free State army was successful and the war ended in 1923 (2008, Coohill 143–144). Coohill suggests that in order to allay the concerns of anti-Treaty republicans, William T. Cosgrave, the President of the executive council of the Irish Free State, introduced a cultural policy in the mid-1920s which made the Irish language compulsory in elementary and secondary education, and in certain professions. Furthermore, the nationalist version of history was taught in schools (2008, 145). According to Coohill:

> Much of this effort coincided with public opinion in the Free State, which increasingly saw Irishness as synonymous with rural life, an agricultural economy and the Catholic religion. (2008, 145)

According to Elliott, in terms of the position of Protestants in the Irish Free State, approximately 100,000 of them left during this period because they felt that they were in a vulnerable position. This meant that by 1926 only 7.4 percent of the total population was Protestant (2009, 216). Elliott further states that there was a denial by Irish nationalists that sectarianism formed an element of its make up or that there was a sectarian motive for the attacks on Protestants and their property (2009, 217). According to Coohill, 'The 1930s and 1940s saw the assertion of final independence of the Irish Free State from any British connection'. As part of the move towards independence the Irish Free State adopted a constitution in 1937 which changed the name of the state to Éire (Ireland) (Daly 2007, 76). Enshrined in the constitution was the protection of the special status of the Catholic Church in Irish society and the inclusion of clauses laying claim to the whole territory of Ireland. The legal system and social policy were adapted to reflect Catholic doctrine on issues such as abortion, contraception and divorce (Coohill, 151–152).

---

16 Rather than incorporate the newly created state into the United Kingdom, the new political union of England, Scotland, Wales and Northern Ireland became the 'United Kingdom of Great Britain and Northern Ireland' (Parekh 2000, 15).

Some Protestants in the Republic of Ireland were unhappy about the influence of the Catholic Church. According to Hennessey, unionists in Northern Ireland feared that any move towards a united Ireland would lead to 'Rome Rule', especially after the Irish Free State adopted their constitution (2005, 9). As one respondent said:

> … and I understand the fear really of 'Home Rule is Rome rule' from the point of view of Protestants because Catholics being in the majority, the educational system has been dominated by Catholics and also the health system …

Another respondent commented that:

> So there was that mentality that we mustn't let our young people mix with anybody, with Catholics, or they're gone to the Catholic Church, the children are gone to the Catholic Church and it [Protestantism] will diminish.

1.5 *Northern Ireland*

Elliott argues that the new Northern Ireland state was inherently unstable from its inception due to the sizable Catholic minority which was 34 per cent of the population and opposed to 'the new political situation' (2009, 216). In particular, people in counties Fermanagh and Tyrone, which had a higher proportion of Catholics than the rest of Northern Ireland, wanted to remain part of the Irish Free State (Berresford Ellis 2004, 8). According to David McKittrick and David McVea, despite the boundaries of the new state being drawn to ensure a Protestant majority, there was ongoing insecurity within the Protestant community about the British government's long-term commitment to maintaining the Union (2001, 4).

McKittrick and McVea argue that the new parliament was dominated by the Unionist party and that there was no incentive to protect and develop the interests of Catholics in Northern Ireland (2001, 6). This was particularly reflected in political representation, public housing allocation and access to higher education and employment (Coogan 1995, 26). One example of how the new state sought to promote the interests of the Protestant community was in local elections. Proportional representation was abolished in 1922 and the first past the post voting system was introduced: this disadvantaged Catholics who were in the minority. This, combined with the partisan redrawing of local authority boundaries (known as 'gerrymandering'), led to Derry passing from nationalist to unionist control despite a clear Catholic majority in the city (McKittrick and

McVea 2001, 8). McKittrick and McVea argue that during the 1920s and 1930s the British government stood back from Northern Ireland, leaving the Unionist party in control, and that many Catholics refused to participate in the political process (2001, 9).

Following the establishment of the Republic of Ireland, an Ireland Act (1949) was passed in Westminster which included a clause that there would be no change in the constitutional status of Northern Ireland without the consent of the Northern Ireland parliament (Coogan 1995, 24). Coogan asserts that the principle of consent was crucial in terms of the lack of political and social progress for the Catholic minority, because it reinforced the power of the Unionist party to veto any change in the *status quo* (1995, 24). As Berresford Ellis argues, the partition of Ireland was therefore in reality given permanent status (2004, 8).

1.6 *The 'Troubles'*

This protracted period of violent sectarian upheaval, at times spreading to the Republic of Ireland and towns and cities in England, began in the late 1960s in Northern Ireland. The 'Troubles' and the response of the authorities to the breakdown of law and order impacted on people's lives in a number of ways; for example, these respondents spoke about their experience of contact with the security forces:

> Well, it's interesting looking back at that time – it was a very militarized place. Walking into town you would have gone through one, two, three, four, possibly five army checkpoints. Most of the time – frisked down. In 1970 I was placed in Bangor because that's where we were living. It's amazing to kind of try and describe it. It's like a world apart. Bangor is only 12, 14 miles from Belfast but it might as well have been two, three hundred miles from Belfast. Belfast was exploding into this kind of turmoil at that stage and yet we were living in the relative comfort of a house in Bangor and only certain interludes actually intruded on that. One example – the army were chasing some people in a car with explosive material in it and they actually abandoned the car in the road that we were living in. So we all had to move out of our houses and during the course of the night we had to take our two children out …

The sense of being in a world apart, mentioned in the previous quotation was highlighted when Andy Pollak gathered evidence for '*The Opsahl Report on Northern Ireland*'. Pollak concluded that middle-class people who were not working for the military, police or prison service had a low risk of being harmed by the conflict and stated that the violence predominantly impacted on the lives of people in deprived, working class urban communities and those living in border areas (1993, 9). Several respondents referred to the class-based and localised nature of the conflict. Here are two more examples from the interviews:

> The 'Troubles' are one thing but the actual environment that people lived in, I think, is well obviously closely aligned to the 'Troubles', and north/west Belfast at that time was reckoned in a whole series of criteria to be one of the most deprived areas in western Europe. The standard of housing was deplorable. Unemployment was running at something like 50 to 60 per cent. And most of that was long term unemployment amongst men, particularly Catholic areas more than the Protestant areas.

> I was living in this nice little bubble in the middle of county Armagh very comfortable and not very affected by the 'Troubles'... In some ways I can't really remember any events that affected me personally ... and that's different when I get to be in my business life because it started to really affect us ... I think a lot of Northern Ireland kids in the middle classes particularly were. It was the working classes ... the working class people, particularly in Northern Ireland, have been right through the 'Troubles'. It was they who were at each other's throats generally and they were the ones who were moving out of ... so Protestants were getting out of Catholic areas or vice versa but those were all working class areas.

By 1998, when the constitutional settlement known as the Good Friday Agreement had been negotiated, more than 3,600 people had been killed and 30,000 injured (Fitzduff, and O'Hagan 2009, 1).

1.7 *The Impact of Sectarianism on Irish Quakerism*

Sectarianism in the two Irish states has also had an impact on the identity of Friends. Findings from my fieldwork show that their identities are 'hybrid' and complex and that this is reflected in the cultural, political and theological spectrum of the Society. These diverse identities have resulted in tensions over key issues that highlight different traditions within Ireland Yearly Meeting.

The conflict and social upheaval endemic in the country from the early settlement of Friends in Ireland was a challenge to their peace testimony which is a fundamental aspect of Quaker theology. The Society's response was to try to maintain a low key presence in their local communities and remain apart from involvement in sectarian-related conflict. For example, Friends were instructed by their National Meeting to destroy their weapons and avoid taking sides during the 1798 Rebellion, although they gave practical assistance to those affected by hostilities between the different groups.

Quakers faced restrictions on their participation in society, like other Dissenters and Roman Catholics, because of the penal laws. Quakers also experienced further persecution because of their theological beliefs which led to their refusal to conform to certain social conventions or to pay tithes. They developed ways of supporting each other and imposing discipline by setting up an organisational structure based on the model introduced by George Fox. In time, as restrictions on Dissenters were relaxed, Friends occupied a position in society as merchants, in trade and in the professions – they were seen as part of the Protestant community but not in the mainstream of Protestantism.

The role of Quakers during the period of the 'Great Famine' was highly significant for the future standing of Friends. The provision of non-sectarian relief during the famine years led to Friends having a reputation for neutrality which proved to be useful for those involved in 'Troubles'-related work. From the late nineteenth century onwards, Irish Friends began to move away from a position of detachment towards the 'Irish Question', when a small number of Friends supported the Irish Home Rule campaign and then later expressions of Irish Republicanism. However, the majority of Friends supported the Union and were concerned about the influence of the Roman Catholic Church if the Home Rule campaign was successful. The issue of whether it was possible or desirable to maintain political 'neutrality' came to the fore again during the 'Troubles' in Northern Ireland, when the complex identity of the Society was highlighted and challenged by the sectarian nature of the conflict.

1.8 *Terminology, Language and Historical 'Balance'*

The subject of politically 'loaded' language is part of the context for understanding Irish Quakerism because like other people in the two Irish states, Friends also make choices about how to express certain concepts and identity categories. One example is the decision whether to describe someone as 'Catholic' or 'Roman Catholic'. According to Martin Melaugh and Brendan Lynn:

> The term 'Roman Catholic' is used frequently in Northern Ireland but more so by members of the Protestant community. Some Catholics are uneasy with the term 'Roman Catholic' as it implies a subservience which does not take account of the historically unique character of the Catholic Church in Ireland. (2005)

Members of the Catholic community in Northern Ireland who support a reunification of Ireland are referred to as 'nationalists'.[17] 'Republicans' have the same aim as nationalists but a number of them subscribe to the view that the use of force is a legitimate strategy to achieve their goals (McCartney 1999, 13). Respondents in my study who described themselves as republican stressed that Republicanism was on a spectrum and positioned themselves as constitutional republicans. This indicates the sensitivities for Quakers of the association of Republicanism with the use of violence which is explored in the publication. Jennifer Todd suggests that the political opportunities for republicans brought about by the Good Friday Agreement of 1998 have come 'at the cost of cognitive dissonance', in the sense that their identity was primarily shaped as a response to British colonialism. Republicans actively participating in the Northern Ireland Assembly have had to come to terms with the new political reality of power sharing arrangements with unionists (Todd 2010, 24).

'Unionists' are members of the Protestant community who support the Union with the United Kingdom, as are 'loyalists'. The latter are associated with paramilitary groups and the use of force to preserve the Union (McCartney 1999, 13). Both unionists and loyalists see their primary national identity as British and many of them are descendants of English and Scottish Protestants who settled in Ireland during the Plantation era from the early seventeenth century onwards, mainly but not exclusively in the north-east corner of the Island (McCartney 1999, 13). According to McCartney, not all Catholics and Protestants fit neatly into the categories outlined above and some have rejected the automatic association between their religion and a particular political affiliation (1999, 13). Some Catholics are unionists and have positive feelings about being part of the United Kingdom, mainly because of the introduction of the welfare state after the Second World War and the more liberal social policies in Northern Ireland compared to the Republic of Ireland. A smaller number of Protestants are nationalists and favour a united Ireland[18] (Liechty and Clegg 2001, 33, McCartney 1999, 13).

Depending on an individual's cultural identity, Northern Ireland could be referred to as 'Ulster' and the 'Province' (the six counties of Northern Ireland are in the province of Ulster). These are terms used by some unionists and

17 Lower case is used when referring to members of the nationalist/republican and unionist/loyalist communities. Upper case is used for political parties or movements etc.

18 In the past many prominent nationalist leaders were Protestant; for example, Theobald Wolfe Tone, who was one of the leaders of the United Irishmen and fought alongside Catholics to bring about an independent Irish parliament in the unsuccessful 1798 Rising (Frayling 1996, 144).

loyalists that are generally unacceptable to nationalists and republicans. The 'six counties' and the 'north of Ireland' are expressions commonly used by nationalists and republicans which are unacceptable to those in the unionist community because, for example, the term 'north of Ireland' places emphasis on the geographical location of that part of Ireland, rejection of partition and an aspiration for a united Ireland (Melaugh and Lynn 2005). Respondents also reflected these nuances of language in the way they referred to 'northern' and 'southern' Friends and the 'north and south of Ireland' (the latter were mainly Friends from the Republic of Ireland).

The significance of language and how it links with identity is also illustrated by the name the two communities give to the second major city, in the north west of Northern Ireland. Nationalists and republicans usually refer to it as Derry and members of the unionist and loyalist community call it Londonderry (Melaugh and Lynn 2005). In the 1980s it acquired the nickname 'Stroke City'[19] and then more recently 'Legenderry'.[20] Respondents shared instances of how the use of, for example, Derry or Londonderry, caused tensions between Friends because this highlighted their different cultural and political backgrounds. During my fieldwork and when writing this publication I also had to navigate these choices of language and terminology. For example, in discussing the two Irish states I refer to the Republic of Ireland (or the Republic for short) and Northern Ireland because they are recognised political entities.

I argue that formulating a 'balanced' historical account involves making choices about what is to be included in the narrative and where the emphasis is placed in discussion of historical figures and events. This process is particularly

---

19 Gerry Anderson, a presenter on Radio Foyle, a local BBC radio station, described how he came to call his hometown 'Stroke City'. Anderson relates how in 1984 the ruling nationalist Social Democratic and Labour Party (SDLP) changed the name of the city council from Londonderry to Derry. This angered unionists who continued using the name Londonderry. The BBC issued a directive to its presenters saying that Londonderry should be used when introducing the city and then Derry subsequently. Anderson decided to use the expression Derry stroke Londonderry. This was then shortened to 'Stroke City'. Anderson also recounted how people who were stopped at army checkpoints and asked where they were going to, could easily be identified as nationalists or unionists by how they answered and this tended to make nationalists a target for extra questioning by the Crown Forces (Anderson, 2000).

20 During a visit to Derry in 2012 I noticed that the buses from the airport had Legenderry written on the side of them. I asked about the significance of this and was told that it was to help reclaim the name of the city from sectarian overtones ahead of Derry-Londonderry being the City of Culture in 2013.

challenging in situations of violent sectarian conflict where communities have different versions of their country's history. According to Liechty and Clegg, what matters is not the historically accurate 'facts' about what happened in the past but the meanings that individuals and communities give to these events in the present time (2001, 64–65). John Tosh and Sean Lang refer to the development of a community's collective memory, experience and sense of identity; they argue that in Northern Ireland there is a fragmentation of this memory due to different claims about the past and the way that significance is attached to past events by each community (2006, 2). According to Tosh and Lang, this results in a lack of shared 'social' memory of the past which will lead the communities in conflict to emphasis some events and exclude others (2006, 3).

In order to take these factors into account in terms of providing a 'balanced' narrative, I consulted a range of authoritative sources that reflect the perspectives of different traditions, such as the Conflict Archive on the Internet site (CAIN) based in the International Conflict Research Institute, Ulster University. To broaden my understanding of Unionism which was less developed than the nationalist/republican perspective, I focused particularly on sections of the literature that explore the historical and political background of the unionist/loyalist community, strands of anti-Catholicism within Unionism, and unionists' identity as British citizens. For example, I consulted the work of Feargal Cochrane about the ideology of Ulster unionists (1997) and Marianne Elliott's examination of the differences between Catholic and Protestant theology and its significance in the Irish context (2009).

1.9 *Theoretical Framework*

The theoretical framework for this study draws on the literature about social identity formation and in particular contested identities. For example, Claire Mitchell (2006) proposes that personal identity is hybrid and multi-layered; these layers or strands of identity include identity labels such as gender, class, religion, nationality, cultural heritage and occupation. There is a particular focus in the publication on Jennifer Todd's work (2005, 2010, 2012 and Todd et al 2006) on sectarianism and oppositional identities in Ireland. In the context of Quakerism there is limited scholarship about how Quaker identity has been sustained without a specific creed or doctrine to act as a focus for unity; for example, Peter Collins (2009). I draw extensively on my own study, Maria Kennedy (2016), which explored the nature and complexity of Irish Quaker identity. My work is primarily a sociological study using qualitative research methods and situated within the historical context of the development of the two Irish states.

1.10 *Specific Case Study of Irish Quakers – Some Key Themes*

Irish Friends' identities are hybrid and complex and this is reflected in the culture of the Society. For example, there are Friends who describe themselves as Quaker (not Protestant), liberal, republican and culturally-Catholic, whereas others identify as Quaker, evangelical and unionist. I discuss two of the main strands of hybrid identity in this publication (political and theological) with examples of how these play out. I suggest that these diverse identities have resulted in tensions over key issues that highlight different traditions within Ireland Yearly Meeting (IYM).

I explore how IYM prioritises what I term relational unity at a corporate level, and have developed a model of complex identity management. In other words the focus is on avoiding hurt by not emphasising differences between Friends. For example, there was evidence from the interviews that a different relationship to being Quaker was demonstrated by some Friends, in particular over claims that Quaker theology is about the testimonies (by liberal Friends) or about traditional Christian beliefs (by evangelical Friends). A number of evangelical Friends were concerned about the theological direction of the Society, suggesting that it was moving away from its Christian roots to be more about social activism than a belief in biblical truths and salvation through relationship with Jesus Christ. I analyse how these differences between Friends were managed at a corporate level to maintain the unity of the organisation in section 5.

I argue that although agreement about what constitutes Quakerism was problematic within the organisation because of the factors outlined previously, some Friends negotiated and transcended aspects of their identities so that in the wider society the label 'Quaker' could function as a meta-identity or 'third way'.

2 Historical Context (Ireland and Quakers)

This section outlines the history and settlement of Quakers in Ireland from the mid-seventeenth century onwards and examines how Irish Quakers positioned themselves as part of a community of Dissenters. This section considers how the Religious Society of Friends sought to navigate the many political and social upheavals that they encountered and explores how Friends responded to these challenges. It suggests that this process of navigation and accommodation is a continuous theme of Irish Quaker history in contemporary times. It examines the emergence of significant theological and political strands of Irish Quakerism in the nineteenth century and the impact this had on the Society. The response of Quakers to Irish Nationalist movements is then discussed. The 'Troubles' era (1968–1998) proved to be a major test of Quaker concepts of 'neutrality'. The response of Friends in Ireland to this crisis is explored.

2.1 *The Origins of the Religious Society of Friends in Ireland*

The foundation of Irish Quakerism dates from 1654 when William Edmondson[21] held the first Meeting for Worship in Lurgan, County Armagh (Greaves 1997, 28) and then went on to help establish Meetings in the north of Ireland and in Dublin (Kilroy 1994, 83). There were also a number of English missionaries, such as Edward Burrough and Francis Howgill, who were members of a group who became known as the 'Valiant Sixty',[22] who came frequently to Ireland to preach the Quaker message (Douglas 2004, 13). Converts were mainly drawn from the population of English settlers, including those who had been Cromwellian soldiers and had been given parcels of land in Ireland in lieu of payment for military services (Vann and Eversley 1992, 46). According to Audrey Lockhart, many of the soldiers recruited into the new model army were already nonconformists and open to 'convincement' (1988, 67). Wigham asserts that few Friends spoke Irish and this was one of the reasons why native Catholics were hard to preach to and convert (1992, 27–28). It was only in the latter part of the twentieth century that some Catholics became interested in Quakerism – how this development impacted on the Society is explored in section 4.

Kilroy suggests that by 1660, despite all the difficulties they experienced, Quakers had managed to establish 30 Meetings. By 1701 this had grown to 53 (Kilroy 1994, 90). The geographical spread of Quakerism was uneven; Quakers tended to be concentrated in specific parts of Ireland in the provinces of Munster, Leinster and Ulster, in small urban centres and in the major cities of Dublin, Cork, Waterford and Limerick (Vann and Eversley 1992, 47–48). There was no Provincial Meeting in Connaught because it had a very small number of

21 Edmondson was born in Westmoreland, England in 1627 and trained as a carpenter and joiner. He eventually joined Cromwell's army and, according to Wigham, was searching for spiritual direction, when he first became aware of Quakerism (1992, 17). After his marriage to Margaret Stanford, Edmondson decided to move to Ireland, where his brother's regiment was stationed, and became established as a shop-keeper. During his first return trip to England, Edmondson met James Naylor (an early Quaker preacher and missionary) and became 'convinced' (Wigham 1992, 18).

22 'The Valiant Sixty' was a term given to a group of early missionaries who were 'convinced' by George Fox and travelled around spreading the Quaker message. According to Elfrida Vipont, Fox often used valiant as a description in his writings (1975, xiii).

Quakers (Hatton, 1993, 36). Endogamy[23] was strictly enforced and this explains why the regional association with certain Quaker families continued (Harrison 2008, 11). Furthermore, Vann and Eversley state that endogamy led to a trend of dynastic marriage, connecting Quaker families in the north and south of the country (1992, 60). In 1669 George Fox came to Ireland (Wigham 1992, 25). Wigham states that the main outcome of Fox's visit was to confirm the structure of the Religious Society of Friends in Ireland[24] (1992, 26).

According to Kilroy, it was very important that any conflict between Friends be settled within the Society and 'so strong was the desire to maintain unity that those who refused to settle differences within the meeting were disowned' (1994, 96). This also applied to doctrinal disputes; any Quaker who intended to write a religious tract was required to bring it to their Meeting to gain approval. Kilroy argues that the threat of disownment and close supervision of Friends was how the corporate body maintained unity in this period (1994, 96–97). How Friends in contemporary times manage unity is explored in section 5.

2.2 *The Response of Early Friends to Violent Conflict in Ireland*

John Douglas suggests that the first major test of the peace testimony of Friends came during the period of violent conflict in Ireland between 1689 and 1691 known as the Williamite war[25] (2004, 9). Although Friends refused to participate in the war, Greaves states that they pledged their loyalty to James II in 1689, following his proclamation of religious liberty and promise to protect Friends (1997, 144–145). However, Harrison asserts that the natural sympathies of Friends was with William of Orange and although the penal laws that resulted from the Treaty of Limerick in 1691 which marked the formal ending of the war, 'further reinforced sectarian prejudice', Quakers were keen not to be seen as undermining the Protestant Ascendancy that was the outcome of the conflict (2006, 23).

Nevertheless, according to Greaves, many Friends experienced great hardship during the war because of the threat of physical harm, damage to their property and seizure of goods and livestock by militia from both sides (1997, 362–363). Greaves goes on to argue that:

23 Endogamy – where marriage is only permitted within the group (Dandelion 2008b, 131).

24 Provincial Meetings were renamed Quarterly Meetings in 1792 (Religious Society of Friends in Ireland 1971, 4).

25 This became known as the Williamite or Jacobite war because the two protagonists were William of Orange and James II.

> … Friends lived in the shadow of persecution, whether actual or potential, throughout the period, and this cannot have failed to affect their lives both by sharpening the focus between themselves as a separated people and the rest of society and by emphasizing the need for a trenchant organisation to preserve their community and its traditions. (1997, 363)

The next example of how Friends responded to sectarian violence in Ireland occurred towards the end of the eighteenth century. Wigham contends that during the period leading up to the 1798 Rebellion, Friends were concerned not to be placed in a position of taking sides or participating in the conflict (1992, 65). According to Thomas Hancock, this position was criticised as a 'dereliction of civic duties' by loyalists (1844, 25). The National Meeting of 1795 cautioned that 'all Friends to be guarded against entering into contracts, or dealing in any articles which may weaken our Christian testimony (against war)' (Wigham 1992, 65). This was followed up in 1796 when the National Meeting recommended that Friends destroy their weapons, refuse to assist in the military preparations of either side in the conflict and also to give food and shelter to those in need without showing partiality (Punshon 1984,154–155). Douglas suggests that the National Meeting had a clear position that Friends should not be drawn into the conflict, but locally some Friends found it difficult to comply, not so much to take sides, but to protect their families and property (1998, 16). According to Wigham, during the Rebellion Friends in counties Kildare and Wexford (where the fighting was most intense in the south of Ireland) were threatened with violence and their houses were raided, but they continued to help both communities (1992, 65). An example of this is located in Susan Egenolf's work about Protestant women's narratives during the 1798 Rebellion which refers to the response of the Quaker Leadbeater family, who lived in Ballitore, county Kildare. Egenolf observes that the Leadbeaters had close ties with members of the United Irishmen however:

> Despite these partisan associations, their deeper religious commitment was to the principles of equality, friendship, and peace, and they refused to engage in any violent political action. (2009, 218)

In his observation about the identity of the Religious Society of Friends and their position in Irish society, Rynne asserts that by the nineteenth century:

> Irish Quakers … became neither colonist nor colonised. Despite experiencing a form of discrimination familiar to other dissenters, and to Roman Catholics, they remained resolutely loyal to their sovereign. But

> at the same time they sought to travel two paths. The first was an inward one which enabled them to maintain a strong group identity, the second an outward journey which brought them gradually closer to a society initially hostile to their existence upon its periphery. (2008, 12)

The political turmoil of the late eighteenth century also coincided with a period of discordance about the theological direction of the Religious Society of Friends, both in Ireland and other parts of the Quaker world. The impact on Irish Friends is explored in the next section.

2.3 *Theological Divergence in Irish Quakerism*

According to Liechty and Clegg, by the beginning of the nineteenth century the penal laws were seen as having failed to achieve one of their primary objectives: to create a Protestant society in Ireland by encouraging Catholics and Dissenters to convert to the Established Church (2007, 86). By this period evangelicalism as a means of conversion was viewed as more acceptable and achievable. Consequently, the Evangelical Society was formed in Ulster in 1798 which spearheaded a very active reform movement (Liechty and Clegg 2007, 86). However, the census of 1861 showed that there had been no significant change in denominational allegiance, indicating that these attempts to convert Catholics had largely failed and that the evangelical crusaders 'were far more successful at revitalising their own Protestant Churches' (Liechty and Clegg 2007, 91).

Wigham suggests that the origins of the theological diversity within the Religious Society of Friends in Ireland happened in the late eighteenth century, when there was a sense of spiritual decline in Irish Quakerism which continued until the 'evangelical revival' mentioned above (1992, 67). According to Wigham, this period marked the beginning of a split between Friends who emphasised the workings of the spirit and those who tended be more scripturally based in their spirituality (1992, 67). Douglas also refers to Friends being affected by the political tensions of the time (just prior to the 1798 Rebellion) and disunity about theology and Quaker discipline (1998, 16).

A sign that evangelicalism was in the ascendancy is evidenced by the treatment of Abraham Shackleton, the clerk of Carlow Monthly Meeting, who was disowned in 1801. Shackleton had been in dispute with his Meeting because he had refused to do readings from the revised Queries[26] which referred to the

26 Advices and queries are texts in the Quaker anthology which give Friends guidance about the conduct of their lives (Quakers in Britain 2013, 1.01.).

Bible as 'Holy' (Alexander 2006, 49). The theological direction of Quakerism also troubled a number of other Friends and several were disowned or resigned from the Society (Wigham 1992, 69).

Harrison asserts that the 'evangelical revival' had a profound impact on the Religious Society of Friends stating that:

> The ideology of evangelicalism (from the mid-19th century) was slowly absorbed into the Quaker ethos, but modified by Quaker Quietist, liberal and communal values. During the 1860s the discovery of this new Biblically-informed access to the living spiritual life galvanised the Society and led to an increasing Quaker population in Ulster, while in Leinster and Munster the Quaker population dwindled.[27] (2008, 14)

Harrison also makes the point that the distinctiveness of Quakerism in Ulster may also be linked to the influence of Presbyterianism which was a more active force in the north of Ireland than in the rest of the country (2008, 13).

Friends made an important contribution to relief efforts during the time of the 'Great Famine'. Hatton argues that Friends were critical of the British government's approach to famine relief. When the 'Great Famine' occurred they decided to set up their own relief scheme (1993, 58). Robin Goodbody also suggests that Friends were concerned that the relief measures set up by the government would not be effective without their practical and financial support (1995, 3). The Central Relief Committee of the Society of Friends was established in Dublin in 1846 to co-ordinate the work.

According to Goodbody, there was an early recognition of the difficulty of linking with other parts of Ireland, particularly Connaught, which had no Provincial Meeting and where the impact of the famine was very acute (1995, 4). Goodbody also refers to a corresponding meeting convened by Meeting for Sufferings[28] in London in order to consider a response to the crisis and seek the advice of Irish Friends. It was decided to set up a relief committee, with Quakers in England focusing on fundraising and those in Ireland on relief

27 The concentration of evangelical Friends in Northern Ireland continues to the present time although there are many liberal Quakers in Belfast and a smaller number of evangelicals in the Republic of Ireland (from interviews and Elizabeth Duke's fieldwork notes).

28 Meeting for Sufferings was founded in London in 1675 with the purpose of assisting Friends experiencing persecution by the authorities for their religious beliefs. In time its focus changed to campaigning and acting as a permanent committee dealing with matters that arose between the Yearly National Meetings of Friends (The Yearly Meeting of the Religious Society of Friends (Quakers) in Britain 2013, 7.01).

distribution (1995, 5). Soup kitchens were established by Quakers in Dublin and Cork, these kitchens became the standard approach for distribution of the soup in other parts of the country (Wigham 1992, 85–86). In time sub-committees were organised 'to handle specific tasks', including committees in the south and south-west of Ireland which managed relief operations in those areas (Goodbody 1998, 28). Friends also made contact with non-Quakers closer to the regions where people were in need of relief and worked with them to operate the soup kitchens and distribute other forms of relief and clothing (Goodbody 1998, 28).

According to Goodbody, by 1847 the need for food and clothing lessened and the focus of the relief committee changed to providing more long-term solutions (1998, 28). At that time the British government had decided to change the system for providing relief and establish their own soup kitchens which would be administered through the poor law unions.[29] This followed the removal of the requirements for admittance to the poor house to receive relief for certain categories of paupers, or for those deemed 'fit' for employment who had previously worked on government sponsored schemes in order to receive food (Goodbody 1998, 28). Quakers did not want to replicate what was being offered and, in addition, they were beginning to run out of funds to continue this form of assistance. It was therefore decided to use the resources available to concentrate on provision for those not entitled to help from the government and to fund projects that would provide people with the means to become more self-sufficient and produce their own food (Hatton 1993, 7).

Hatton suggests that at the time, Quakers considered that their efforts to alleviate the impact of the famine had largely been a failure because they were not successful in persuading the government to bring about radical change to tackle the underlying causes of poverty and deprivation in Ireland (1993, 267). Additionally, the scale of the death toll from the famine and emigration of people from Ireland made it difficult for those involved in relief work to feel positively about their efforts. The perceived failure of influence stemming from the 'Great Famine' was one of the reasons why Quakers were persuaded to enter politics, when Jonathon Pim became the first Irish Friend to enter parliament as a Liberal MP for Dublin in 1865 and continued to campaign for land reform (Goodbody 1998, 32).

29 Ireland was divided into Poor Law Unions for the purpose of providing relief to the destitute and each district was managed by an elected board of guardians. There were strict regulations about who was eligible for relief (Goodbody 1995, 7). In 1847 the government introduced a new Poor Law scheme and a Food Kitchens Act was implemented. This changed the basis of the government provision of relief (Wigham 1992, 87).

However, Goodbody argues that, considering that there were only 3,000 Friends in Ireland at this time, the scale and diversity of their work was remarkable (1998, 32). In addition, one respondent commented that:

> I think historically in the Republic there was considerable recognition for the role Friends played in famine relief, and also I think there may be some recognition for what I would deem, although it's contradictory, Protestant neutrality. Personally I would rather that Friends were neutral between sects but as the majority of people would perceive you – if you were other than RC and a Christian – as being a Protestant ... I do think that certainly the famine recognition has left an impression of Friends in the Republic which is benign.

This observation suggests that there is a corporate Irish memory of the non-sectarian approach of Friends to the provision of relief during the 'Great Famine' which has persisted in contemporary times.

2.4 *The Response of Friends to Irish Nationalism*

Friends' attempts to remain apart from involvement in Irish Nationalism proved to be increasingly difficult during the Home Rule crisis of the 1870s onwards when it became evident that the majority were opposed to Home Rule and wanted to maintain the Union. Philip Ashton contends that, in general, Friends were not opposed to Catholic emancipation. They were concerned about the influence of the Roman Catholic Church in a more autonomous Ireland and some believed that sectarian divisions would intensify (2000, 17). There was a small, politically active group of Friends who were in favour of Home Rule and a smaller number of them went on to support the various Irish nationalist groups that emerged when the outbreak of the First World War delayed the implementation of Home Rule.

After the partition of Ireland in the early 1920s the Religious Society of Friends remained one organisation (Neill 1999, 13). However, the increasingly separate development of the two new political entities (the Irish Free State and Northern Ireland) also began to intensify the pre-existing political and theological differences within the Society (Wigham 1992, 121–122). This meant that with the outbreak of the 'Troubles' in the late 1960s, although there were many examples of cross-community projects developed by Friends in Northern Ireland, it was observed by many respondents that it was problematic for the Society to comment publicly about civil rights issues such as the unequal position of Catholics in the Northern Irish state. Respondents also mentioned that the 'Troubles' were not discussed at Yearly Meetings, and that separate meetings were arranged for Friends who wanted to talk about the political dimension of the conflict. This subject is explored more fully in the next section.

2.5 *Quakers and the 'Troubles'*

Felicity McCartney states that by the time the 'Troubles' started in the late 1960s there were approximately 1,600 Quakers of whom almost half lived in Northern Ireland (2009, 10). Quakers were aware of the inequalities in Northern Irish society through a variety of means. For example, Denis Barritt, a local Friend, co-authored *The Northern Ireland Problem* in 1962 which highlighted the inequalities in Northern Irish society (McCartney 2009, 10). Additionally, there had been meetings of Friends to discuss cross-border issues since the 1950s (Wigham 1992, 149).

McCartney places initiatives by Friends in Ireland in the context of Quaker testimonies, especially the peace testimony. She suggests that much of the work of Quakers during the 'Troubles' echoes the concerns of earlier Friends. For example, as outlined earlier, Quakers already had a reputation for providing relief and support on a non-sectarian basis during the 'Great Famine'. There was evidently a concern by Friends that they should provide assistance when the 'Troubles' began (2009, 10). As an initial response, Quaker Meeting Houses were used to house homeless people bombed out of their homes in sectarian violence in Belfast. This work became the genesis of the Ulster Quaker Service Committee which was set up to co-ordinate the work and offers of help from Quakers in Ireland and other countries. For example, when internment without trial was introduced in 1971, the Visitor's Centre at the Maze Prison was set up; Quaker House in Belfast, 1982–2010, served as a confidential space for dialogue to help facilitate political negotiation; the Quaker Peace Education Project (QPEP) worked with young people in schools to help develop resources and skills in how to resolve disputes peacefully. This project ran from 1986–1994 (McCartney 2009, 10). Jerry Tyrrell was appointed director of the QPEP in 1988 (Farrell 2009, 124) and facilitated the work of a scheme called Education for Mutual Understanding (EMU) which was eventually extended to adults working in community settings (2009, 127–128).

Section 4 explores conflict in the Society about the involvement of Quakers with what were regarded as overtly 'political' matters – an issue that was particularly problematic for some Northern Irish Friends from the evangelical wing of Quakerism. A number of respondents observed that it was important that the first representatives[30] based at Quaker House be Irish Friends, particularly

30 Friends appointed to carry out the work of Quaker House.

from Northern Ireland. This explains why in an article appealing to Friends to support Quaker House, Joan and Billy Sinton (representatives from 1982–1984) mention the difficulty of approaching this work as 'insiders', stating that it is important to be aware of and overcome feelings and prejudices and suggest that some Friends struggled with this challenge. They go on to say that the work of Quaker House:

> Is not an underhand movement to 'sell out' or to undermine faiths rather it is an effort to achieve the security, stability and Christian standards which we feel are our due. To achieve this we are prepared to meet and try and understand those of different points of view. Where we meet the spirit of reconciliation, we encourage it. Where there is fear and bitterness, we try, in an unobtrusive way, to spread the gospel of love and forgiveness. (1984, 4)

Ann Bennett states that in 1995 there was a major review of the work of Quaker House by Clem McCartney, who interviewed users of the project. McCartney concluded that there was a need to continue with the work and referred to the possible contribution of Quaker House to changes in the wider society in 'offering a quiet, non judgemental [sic] space for individuals and groups to explore their own thinking and that of others' (2009, 116). For example, Mo Mowlam (Secretary of State for Northern Ireland, 1997–1999) used Quaker House as a venue for informal, private meetings during the period leading up to the Good Friday Agreement. As Janet and Alan Quilley (representatives at Quaker House, 1993–1999) commented:

> Janet Quilley: She would just relax and we would ask people to come and meet – she wanted to talk to people who might have thoughts about future structures and developments and things. Not necessarily the politicians – [but] academics, people like that.
>
> Alan Quilley: We organised three meals when there were particular people she wanted to meet – we invited [them] to come and chatted and she did what she said in the book [Mowlam's memoirs, *Momentum: The Struggle for Peace, Politics and the People*] we did 'help her to hit the ground running'. We [first] managed to make contact with her when she was at the SDLP conference – she was very accessible.

Although much of the work of Friends was based in or near Belfast there were significant projects elsewhere in Northern Ireland, for example, the Peace and Reconciliation Group (PRG) in Derry. The PRG included English Friends, Diana and John Lampen, who were in the city from 1983–1994 and built on the work and contacts of Will Warren, another English Friend who was active in Derry from the early 1970s, to act as mediators between republicans and the security forces (Moloney 2007, 364). The PRG included former paramilitaries and had contacts with paramilitary organisations. John Lampen refers to the uneasiness of some local people, especially victims of the conflict, about the willingness of the PRG to enter into dialogue with paramilitaries. Lampen contends that it is possible to be sympathetic to all those affected by violence and still remain impartial (2011, 10–11).

Ed Moloney argues that in Derry the main focus of conflict was between the nationalist community and the security forces (2007, 352). The PRG sought to improve relationships between the police, the British army and the local communities, which were at a very low point during the 1980s (Lampen 2011, 12). Lampen suggests that responses to this initiative were also mixed. Some in the Irish Republican Army (IRA) felt positive that attempts were being made to challenge oppressive behaviour by the security forces. Other republicans believed that there should be no contact with what they considered to be an illegitimate force (2011, 12). Arthur Chapman suggests that the involvement of John and Diana Lampen in the PRG and its promotion of tension reducing measures set the scene for the IRA ceasefire in 1994 (2009, 30).

Ann Le Mare asserts that Quaker work contributed to capacity building within Northern Ireland by sharing skills and resources, training people and encouraging participation at local and organisational levels (2009, 152). Le Mare states that Quakers were very responsive to local needs and had the capacity to develop a wide range of initiatives including restorative justice, advocacy work and behind the scenes work with politicians, civil servants and other policy makers to improve communication and understanding (2009, 155). She argues that the work undertaken by Quakers is sustaining and has been taken on by other organisations and has had a considerable impact on the lives of individuals (2009, 158).

The Glencree Centre for Peace and Reconciliation, County Wicklow, founded in 1974 is an example of an initiative of a small ecumenical group including Quakers (Kenny 1998, 3). Friends involved in this project included members of the Bewley family. In discussing the organisation Rachel Bewley-Bateman said:

> There was a group called Working for Peace which started off in Dublin about 1969/70 and Dad and I were both members of that and then they set up a steering committee with a view to getting a place to start the Glencree Centre for Reconciliation.

Glencree was used as a base for the Believer's Enquiry in the 1990s to investigate the role of Christians in building peace in Ireland. Quakers were involved both in the early stages of setting up the Enquiry and also contributing their ideas (Kenny 1998, 3–4).

The Ulster Quaker Service Committee, now Quaker Service, continues its work which currently focuses on support for prisoners and their families through the Monica Barritt Visitors' Centre and Quaker Connections befriending service at Maghaberry Prison, county Antrim, and Quaker Cottage, a cross community family support centre in Belfast.

However, according to Wigham, despite the practical response of Friends to the conflict:

> There was a deep political division within the Society as to the political merits of a united Ireland as opposed to a continued Northern Ireland in union with Britain. Awareness of this division prevented open discussion and the conflict as such was never discussed in the Yearly Meeting. It must be reckoned as a weakness of the Society at the time that, in spite of the anxiety of visiting English Friends to understand and get to the nub of the problem and seek a solution, the troubles in the North were only discussed in special interest groups. (1992, 149)

This difficulty is still apparent today. A respondent observed that:

> Northern Friends do focus on the work of Quaker Service, with quite a high proportion actively involved in its work in the prisons and at Quaker Cottage. (Cuts in Government support has meant the charity needs to use volunteers and Quaker funds more, and this has been achieved). These are practical things that Quakers can do something about, and which are not divisive, so are happily a central focus for Northern Quakers. (personal correspondence, 2019)

3 Identity Theory

Theoretical perspectives related to the formation of social identity suggest that it is either primordial/innate or socially constructed/situational (Coleman and Collins 2004, 4). According to Simon Coleman and Peter Collins, 'the 'primordialist' view emphasises the significance of historical continuities in creating attachments to territory and communities'. For example, in the process of nation building, a 'primordialist' perspective would perceive identity as something that is an innate characteristic arising from membership of a social group, the notion of a shared culture and connection to a territorial domain (2004, 4). According to Murat Bayar, Edward Shils was the first sociologist to use the term primordialism (2009, 1641). Shils' view of how a modern society functions is that:

> It is held together by an infinity of personal attachments, moral obligations in concrete contexts, professional and creative pride, individual ambition, primordial affinities and a civil sense which is low in many, high in some, and moderate in most persons. (1957, 131)

Conversely the social constructivist approach focuses on the ongoing process of identification in relation to self and others and how boundaries are created between groups. It also proposes the notion that identity is more fluid than the primordialist perspective (Coleman and Collins 2004, 4–5).

In their work about evangelical Christians in Northern Ireland Claire Mitchell and Gladys Ganiel (2011) discuss changing concepts of identity which they suggest are drawn mainly from a social constructivist perspective. Richard Jenkins provides a useful definition of this approach. He asserts that:

> social identity is simply – and complexly – a *process* of identification, it is no more, and no less, than *how we know who we are and who other people are*; processually, *the individually unique and the collectively shared have much in common*; identification is always a matter of *relationships of similarity AND difference*; it is also a matter of *internal definition and external definition*: this suggests that *identification can never be unilateral* (any more than self-determination can); *identity is negotiable and changeable, but when identification matters, it really matters*; and, finally, *identification is also a matter of its consequences*, as a process – rather than a 'thing', or an ideal classification – it is inherently practical. (Jenkins 2000a, 6)

Mitchell and Ganiel argue that prior to the 1980s the focus of research was on what were regarded as core identities such as 'class, gender and race'. However, they assert that from the 1990s onwards there was a shift towards understanding 'how people mixed and matched their own individual identities' (2011, 15). Mitchell and Ganiel suggest that sociologists became interested in personal choice and how individuals consciously develop a sense of selfhood through awareness of their different identity categories and roles (2011, 15). They argue that religious identity is therefore very much connected to other aspects of identity (Mitchell and Ganiel 2011, 15).

According to Mitchell and Ganiel, post-modernist theorists of identity such as Bauman (1998) extend the concept of identity fluidity, arguing that there is no core identity; that selfhood is in a state of flux and constantly negotiated depending on external social influences (2011, 16). Stuart Hall asserts that: 'Identities are the points of temporary attachment to the subject positions which discursive practices construct for us' (1996, 6). While Judith Butler proposes that, for example, gender is performed and is therefore a role rather than a core identity, and performative – meaning that it is reproduced through behaviour to give an impression of being a man or a woman and therefore gender is much more fluid than had been assumed (2011).

Mitchell and Ganiel outline a number of arguments against 'free choice' in terms of identity. They assert that certain core categories of race, gender and class are still very influential in the construction of identity and identity formation is relational and influenced by socialisation (2011, 16). Jenkins suggests that there is a degree of continuity and stability of identity, particularly related to what he argues are primary identity categories such as selfhood, which develops during the process of primary socialisation, integrating other primary categories such as gender and ethnicity which are resistant to change. Jenkins stresses, however, that 'primary identifications are neither fixed nor timeless. Identification is something that individuals do, it is a *process*' (2014, 72).

Steph Lawler also locates herself within the social constructivist approach to identity formation. A significant theme of Lawler's work is a critique of 'Western' notions of separation between the 'self' and the social world, and trends towards individualism. Lawler argues that this leads to the creation of a sameness/difference binary which produces patterns of discrimination and privileges some identities over others (2014). Lawler stresses that identity is a process, is interconnected and always relational, arguing that: 'identity itself is a social and collective process and not, as Western traditions would have it, a unique and individual possession' (2014, 2–3). Like Jenkins, Lawler suggests that concerns about identity tend to come to the fore when it is viewed as problematic in some way. This can lead to a tendency to compare more complicated forms of identity with what is seen as unproblematic, as though the latter is normative. Lawler's work challenges assumptions that create a binary between 'unproblematic' and 'problematic' identities and instead focuses on identity-making (2014, 1–2).

Todd et al in their work about identity in Ireland state that it is necessary to take into account both primordialist and social constructivist perspectives because this helps us to understand why ethno-national identity and oppositional identities persist when they are viewed in the context of group belonging and social ties (2006, 324). As Todd et al assert, it is also important to look at self-categorisation of identity and how individuals understand how their identity is formed. For example, some may tend towards being 'naïve primordialists' who see their identity as being innate, largely fixed and inherited (2006, 324). According to Todd et al, these two main strands of thinking about ethno-national identity become particularly relevant during periods of social and national change when analysing the persistence of ethno-national conflict (2006, 324–325).

My work is mainly located within the social constructivist perspective of identity and the literature provides a useful frame of reference for analysing findings from the interviews for this publication. Themes such as the impact of family and broader social influences on identity, for example, how individuals negotiate internal identity categories such as political, cultural and theological labels (Jenkins) and the privileging of certain categories (Lawler) are considered within this perspective. The argument proposed by Todd, that it is necessary to recognise both primordial and social constructivist perspectives to account for the persistence of identity-related conflict, contributes to my analysis of sectarianism and the impact on identity.

3.1 *Contested Identity in Ireland*

The underlying causes of Irish sectarianism are highly contested in the Academy. For example, Steve Bruce (2009) and Claire Mitchell (2006) stress the importance that religion and religious beliefs had on the creation of sectarianism and conflict between the nationalist and unionist communities following the partition of Ireland. However, other commentators such as Pamela Clayton (1998) place more emphasis on the impact of English colonial policy on Ireland in institutionalising sectarianism as do Kevin Toolis (1995) and David Miller (1998), who focus particularly on the significance of colonialism and the policy of successive British governments in Northern Ireland as explanations for the outbreak of the 'Troubles'. I argue that Liechty and Clegg's (2001) perspectives on Irish sectarianism can be seen as representing a more nuanced approach. They contend that sectarianism is multi-layered and complex and suggest that it is important to be wary of reductionist or over-simplistic explanations, for example, that it is all to do with colonialism or any other single factor.

Elliott's work examines the impact, potency and difficulties that people have of 'opting out' of sectarianism. She argues that sectarianism was experienced by people on a personal, social and political level and was not just restricted to Northern Ireland but impacted on people throughout the island of Ireland (2009, 5–6). Elliott suggests that people within the sectarian divide will often be unaware of how distorted their perspectives are, holding rigid notions of identity and projecting negative views of the other community. This way of thinking is then passed on through the generations (2009, 5). Elliott concludes that sectarianism has proved to be a more potent force than social class and explains why various attempts to build alliances between working class Protestants and Catholics in the 1930s and 1960s failed (2009, 5).

In my discussion of the complex identity of respondents, I draw on Mitchell's proposition that identity is 'hybrid'. Mitchell refers to identity as being multi-layered; these layers or strands of identity include factors such as gender, class, cultural heritage and occupation. Mitchell suggests that some aspects of our identity may come to the fore in certain situations 'because we take our cues from the people around us' (2006, 12). Todd's work about identity in Ireland came after the Good Friday Agreement[31] and I draw on her research as my main theoretical perspective, comparing her research with my findings about the identity of Quakers in Ireland. Todd's work is about oppositional identity and sectarianism in Ireland and looks at how this functions and is maintained. Todd explores religious divisions (Catholic and Protestant), identity formation and change and she compares how these operate in both Irish states. Todd's research looks at the impact of the different social and political structures in Ireland (north and south) on religious distinctions and national identity. She examines the persistence of conflict based on ethno-national identity and why this form of oppositional identity is so deeply embedded, particularly in Northern Ireland (Todd 2005, 2010, 2012 and Todd et al 2006).

The following is a summary of Todd's main findings and arguments. For example, Todd found that self-categorisation is much more nuanced in both parts of Ireland than a simplistic Protestant/Catholic binary. There were markedly different responses in the Republic of Ireland and Northern Ireland when respondents were asked to describe themselves. In the Republic the research found that the majority of respondents from a Catholic background were less likely to mention their religious affiliation or national identity than those born elsewhere, had previous lived in or were familiar with Northern Ireland or were part of the Protestant minority. Todd suggests that where a group is in the majority and supported by state institutions, national identity is often taken for granted as the default or banal position. I found that respondents in my

31 Jennifer Todd led a large-scale research study in both of the Irish states between 2003 and 2006. This study generated a number of journal articles and papers, some solely authored by Todd and others by Todd and other researchers involved in the study. When talking generally about the research I refer to Todd's findings. When discussing specific aspects of the study I refer to Todd or Todd et al as appropriate.

study from a Catholic background (all were in the Republic) were more likely to mention this and talked about remaining culturally Catholic.

Todd states that some Protestants in the Republic felt that they had to negotiate or signal their background/identity in their interactions with others. Todd argues that despite the mechanisms in place in both parts of Ireland to tackle institutional discrimination, there are still 'symbolic boundaries' that impact on how people participate in society as equal citizens. These boundaries are different in each of the Irish states. For example, in the Republic respondents from Todd's study mentioned that one boundary related to feeling part of Irish culture – some from non-Catholic backgrounds felt like 'outsiders' excluded from certain aspects of Irish society. These factors built up a picture of how people are classified as belonging to or excluded from the Irish nation. In particular, to be English in the Republic is still regarded by some as being an 'outsider' more so than many other groups. Todd suggests that this can only be overcome by strong efforts on the part of these individuals to participate fully in society and embrace 'Irish' ways of interacting.

Todd found that in Northern Ireland people from both communities were more likely to disclose their religious affiliation and national identity than those in the Republic; although in Northern Ireland a significant minority stated that due to the sensitivities of the subject they preferred not to talk openly about their background. Some people avoid self-categorisation as a way of side stepping the sectarian nature of these labels. Todd's research shows that religion continues to be an important factor in the political outlook and voting patterns of many people in Northern Ireland. Conversely I found that some of my respondents in Northern Ireland voted for non-sectarian or nationalist parties. Others found different forms of political activism such as single-issue campaigns as an alternative to sectarian-based party politics and this concurred with my findings.

Todd argues that Northern Ireland has different boundaries which act as triggers of contestation, for example, religion, nationality and political affiliation which at times join together as a major divisive factor. Todd found that identity can be 'thick' or 'thin' depending on how deeply embedded a person's sense of identity is. The more embedded the harder it is for individuals to change their sense of identification because of the effort involved and impact on relationships. Todd suggests that in Northern Ireland it is possible to detect a movement away from cultural identity in both communities to what Todd calls a 'thinner state-centred identity' with some seeing themselves as Northern Irish rather than British or Irish. This view is supported by Kevin McNicholl who argues that Northern Irish has the potential to act as a cross-community identity (2019, 27). This finding chimed with an observation by one of my respondents who said that liberal Friends in the urban areas referred to themselves as Northern Irish. However, many of the evangelical Friends embedded in the Unionist, rural areas of Northern Ireland had a British identity – and this was linked to difficult memories from the Troubles era (personal correspondence, 2019).

Todd goes on to assert that Protestants in Northern Ireland have had the possibility of developing more hybrid identities than Catholics because of the wider variety of ways that they could describe themselves, e.g. Northern Irish, British, Ulster-Scots, but that this is not the same as category fluidity or category change, the latter being much more difficult, especially in the Northern Irish context. As Todd asserts:

> … in both the Irish state and Northern Ireland, nationality is important and related to a sense of belonging, of cultural legacy, political loyalty, local tradition and familial history. But where – for Southern Catholics – local belonging, political loyalty, cultural proclivities and familial tradition all feed into a multi-faceted national identity, in Northern Ireland respondents often disaggregate these facets. (2012, 11)

To conclude, in many instances there was an overlap between Todd's research and my findings. However, interviews with Friends in Ireland, informal conversations and attendance at Irish Quaker gatherings have revealed that the 'hybrid' identities of Friends is more complex than that which is revealed in the literature outlined earlier. Irish Quakers have a diverse range of views in matters related to religion, national identity and political affiliation. These positions did not follow a simple north/south divide but are in part a reflection of a theological division between liberal and evangelical Quakers. I argue that the concept of 'hybrid' identity can be extended beyond Mitchell's and Todd's definitions to include ways that the category 'Quaker' was consciously employed by some Friends to transcend sectarian divisions and find a middle way between the Catholic and Protestant binary. These findings are a significant aspect of my research and will be discussed fully in the publication and illustrated by the use of case studies and a selection of quotations from the interviews in the next part.

4 Irish Quaker Identity

This section focuses on social identity in Ireland, particularly the identity of Quakers. I introduce a Quaker identity matrix which shows how different forms of identity overlap and relate to each other and can be a source of conflict. I explore the complex nature of the identity of Friends in Ireland in terms of their political and theological hybridity: specifically cultural Catholicism and the evangelical/liberal dimension of Irish Quakerism. I then link findings about social identity in Ireland to specific themes about the identity of Irish Friends by comparing and contrasting my research findings with Todd et al's. Included is an exploration of the response of Friends to sectarianism and how individual respondents negotiated and transcended different aspects of their identity. I do this by presenting the main themes from the interview data; these themes are illustrated by two case studies to demonstrate the nature of personal identity in the Irish Quaker context. I then focus on the corporate identity of IYM and the impact of individual hybrid identities on the organisation.

4.1 *Quaker Identity Matrix*

Irish Friends are small in number. In 2010 there were a total of 2141 members and attenders in the Religious Society of Friends in Ireland, including children under the age of 18. Ulster Quarterly Meeting (QM) which covers Northern Ireland has the largest number of adult Friends of the three QMs with 899 (Yearly Meeting of Friends in Ireland 2010). The diverse nature of this small religious group is illustrated by the 22 identity labels gathered from the 15 interviews I carried out. They have been loosely divided into two categories: political/cultural and theological. As I have indicated in the last row of Table 2, one category fits both headings. I outline the reasons why this is later in the section.

TABLE 2 Identity labels

Political/Cultural	**Theological**
Nationalist/Republican	Dissenter
Culturally-Catholic	'Birthright'
Irish	Evangelical
British/Irish	Christo-centric
English	Quaker by 'convincement'
Working-class background	Liberal
No label	Christian
Socialist/Feminist	Born Again Christian
Gay man	Humanist
Irish speaker	Exploring mysticism
	Seeker
Quaker not Protestant	Quaker not Protestant

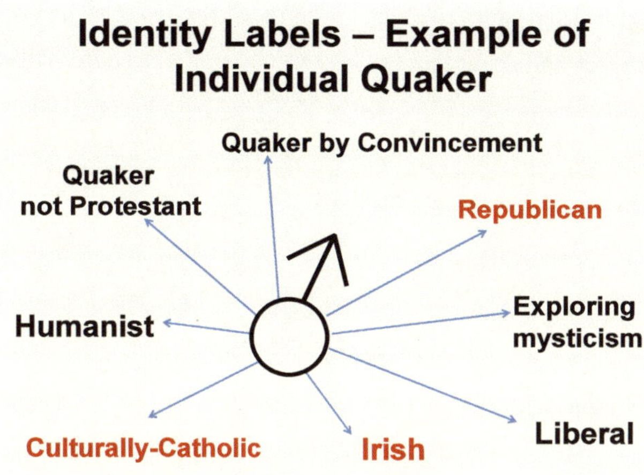

FIGURE 1 Example of an individual identity matrix

Figure 1 gives an example of one individual Friend's somewhat complex 'hybrid' identity – red represents political/cultural identity, black theological position. This respondent is a Quaker by 'convincement' and from a Catholic, nationalist/republican background on the liberal spectrum of Quakerism who is exploring mystical forms of spirituality. He rejected the label Protestant and was very clear that he remains culturally-Catholic. The different identity labels point to a possible conflict of identity; these themes will be explored more fully in the case studies. There have been an increasing number of people from a Catholic background becoming Quakers in recent years which has had an impact on the culture of the Society.

Figure 2 shows some of the identity labels relating to four of the evangelical Friends that I interviewed. The distinction between those from Quaker families ('birthright' Friends) and Quakers by 'convincement' is marked – and linked to the early Quaker dynastic families who were important in holding the Society together after Ireland was partitioned. Dissenters are Friends who emphasis their different roots from mainstream Protestantism, that is, from the dissenting or nonconformist tradition. The respondent (labelled C) who described herself as Christo-centric[32] is possibly avoiding the Quaker evangelical and liberal binary which has caused some tension in the Society. The arrows in the diagram show connections between three of the evangelical Friends and concerted attempts to build bridges with liberal Friends, particularly by the person at the bottom right of the diagram (labelled D). The respondent who described himself as a Quaker fundamentalist (labelled B) seemed to be less

32 Christo-centric – having Christ at the centre.

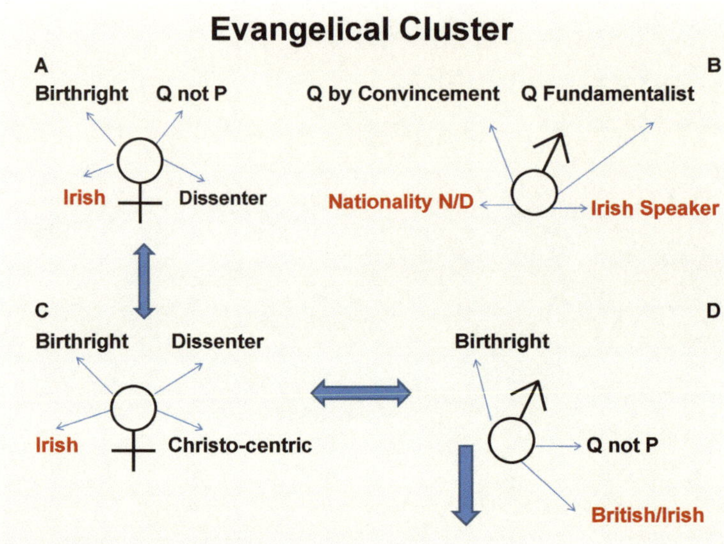

FIGURE 2 Identity matrix – evangelical Quakers

connected to the other evangelical Friends. He expressed a strong opinion that the Society is straying too far from its theological roots. This respondent was not willing to disclose his national identity and articulated his deep attachment to the Irish language.

A quotation from a 'birthright' Friend illustrates the complexity of her identity and sense of being in a very small minority in the Republic of Ireland:

> I'm Irish. I'm in a minority because I'm not Catholic. I'm in a minority because I don't like being called a Protestant, I'm a Dissenter. I'm in a minority because I am a Member of the Religious Society of Friends. I'm in a minority because I'm an evangelical Irish Friend and I'm quite happy with it.

Liberal Friends used a variety of terms to describe themselves. For example, one mentioned being a born again Christian when they discovered Quakerism but not in the sense of being evangelical. The respondents who described themselves as Republican or from a Republican background (labelled A and D) represented a spectrum of political perspectives, from a background in the paramilitary tradition to a constitutional one. Some respondents commented that the Religious Society of Friends has a mainly middle-class membership and those with a different class background tended to emphasise this difference as evidenced by reference to w-c (working class) backgrounds (labelled B and D).

Thomas Tweed asserts that religion can facilitate the crossing of social space, for example, in terms of class (2006, 134). However, for some Irish Friends joining a predominantly middle-class grouping caused them to feel uncomfortable about this aspect of Quakerism. A desire to challenge the assumption that all Quakers were middle-class was part of the motivation for one respondent's (labelled D) decision to be interviewed, as the following quotation shows:

> One of the reasons when I received the email that [I thought] maybe it's time to talk, because the perception is that Quakers are solely a middle-class cohort who are all out of the same mould, well I'm not part of that and I wasn't part of that.

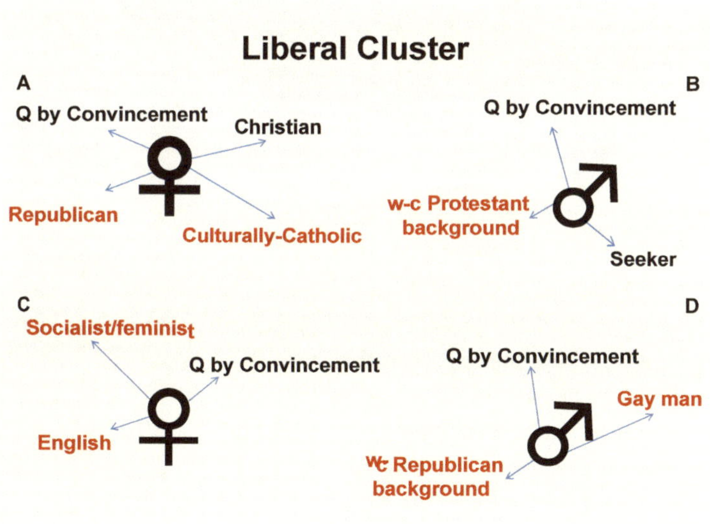

FIGURE 3 Identity matrix – liberal Quakers

Figure 4 shows what happens when all these identity labels are put together and demonstrates the complexities and potential conflict of these identities. In the matrix there appears to be a number of 'oppositional' identity labels. For example, at the top of the diagram, separated from the others, is the category Unionist/Protestant which contrasts with 'Quaker not Protestant'; this is an example of how Friends within the Yearly Meeting perceived each other. None of the respondents interviewed described themselves as unionist or Protestant,

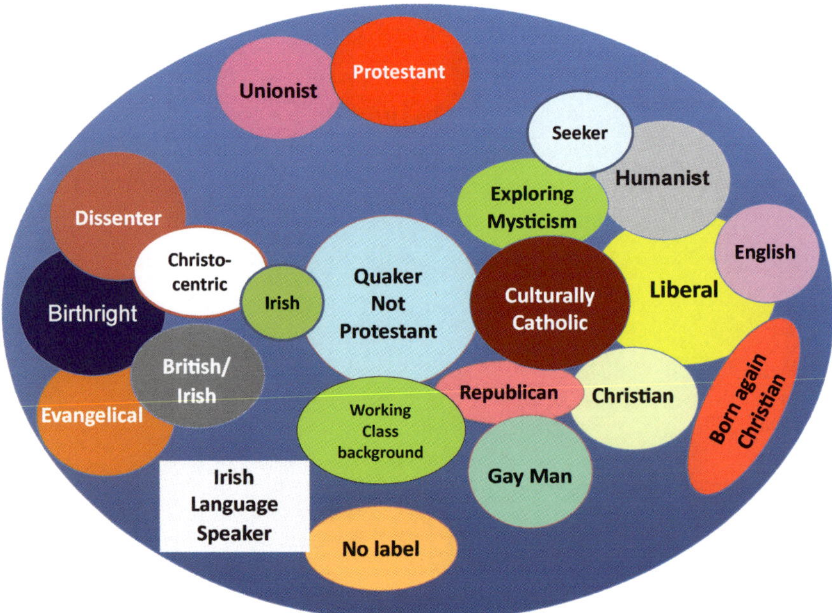

FIGURE 4 Quakers in Ireland: identity matrix

but in the interviews there were many references to evangelical Friends in the rural areas of Northern Ireland being identified with the unionist community around them. Some Friends felt that this tradition had been in the ascendancy within Irish Quakerism until fairly recently. Other potential binary categories include Irish/English and evangelical/liberal.

In recent years there has been a shift from political differences in the Society to contention about homosexuality and same sex relationships. This has caused great tension between those Friends who are more biblically-based in their theology and those using the language of the testimonies to truth and equality. One respondent shared his experience of 'coming out' to other Quakers:

> One of the things that Quakerism teaches you is honesty and the importance of truth. It's a very big thing for Quakerism and it was one of the things that it taught me, and so for years I grappled with this whole concept of truth and the importance of being true … But you can only – you can't be truthful to the world unless you're truthful to yourself … and I spent a good many years trying to deal with the issue of being truthful to myself and one of the outcomes of it was that I came out as a gay man and that was a particularly – it turned out to be subsequently particularly difficult in my Meeting – very difficult and very uncomfortable.

The way that IYM has managed conflict related to the different political and theological backgrounds of Friends is explored more fully in section 5.

The next section compares Todd's findings about disclosure of identity and 'symbolic distinctions' with the findings from my study. Changes in identity content and category and challenges to sectarianism are covered in the individual case studies.

4.2 *Disclosure of Identity*

In terms of disclosure of religious identity, one of the common themes that came out strongly from the identity matrix is that all of the respondents described themselves as 'Quaker not Protestant', hence the central place of this label in Figure 4. This finding is related to the identity label Protestant being 'loaded' in the Irish context and also because Quakerism came out of the dissenting tradition. Protestantism is not just a religious label, it is also a political category associated with the Protestant Ascendancy and British colonialism and that is why 'Quaker' not Protestant appears in both categories in Table 2. The following quotation encapsulates these observations:

> I don't see myself as Protestant, no I don't. I see myself as somebody who seeks to adhere to certain Christian values … I wouldn't tick any boxes. Although when the census forms came in I did write Religious Society of Friends, but I wouldn't tick boxes I wouldn't … we are talking about sectarianism on an island and that's the reason we look at it as we do but we shouldn't have to look at it in those terms. So I just see myself as a person who tries to live according to certain Christian values … But I don't advocate, I don't proclaim what I am or who I am. People will obviously, certainly in the Northern Ireland situation, will perceive me as a nationalist and as a Roman Catholic yes, that doesn't worry me. It worries them possibly more than it worries me. But it can be, it would be difficult for me to live in Northern Ireland.

Findings about disclosure of national identity are more mixed. Some respondents avoided self-categorisation and they tended to be originally from non-Irish backgrounds. For example, one person said that he was unwilling to disclose his nationality, claiming that 'it wasn't important'. Respondents from Catholic backgrounds seemed to have a more banal sense of national identity – conversely 'birthright' Friends highlighted their Irish identity. Other respondents talked about their experience of being English in the Republic and Northern Ireland. This quotation from a respondent in Northern Ireland illustrates the link between nationality and cultural identity:

> It's because I'm an English person with a Protestant background that I did not have the connection with the cultural Protestantism of Northern Ireland – that's linked with Unionism, the Orange Order and Loyal Orders and whatever … There's a significant section of the Protestant community who don't associate with that culture either, but most people who have been brought up Protestant in Northern Ireland would have had, within their family, those connections through cousins, brothers, sisters, uncles, grandparents. I had none of that so that's why I wasn't a cultural Protestant.

The issue of cultural identity is also connected to that of 'symbolic distinctions' and my findings about how they operate in the two Irish states is the subject of the next section.

4.3 *'Symbolic Distinctions/Boundaries'*

My study generally matches Todd's findings about 'symbolic distinctions' and the creation of 'insider' and 'outsider' groups, and also produces new insights about how these issues are addressed. For example, respondents raised as Catholic in the Republic of Ireland seem to have a greater sense of belonging culturally in Irish society than those from different Christian traditions. This concurs with Todd's findings about groups who are in the majority having a more taken for granted or banal identity. However, I found that respondents from a Catholic background were more likely to stress that they remained culturally-Catholic. What seems to be significant in terms of the identity of these respondents is how their cultural-Catholicism is connected to being Irish, despite moving to a different theological affiliation, and to sensitivities about being seen as members of a 'Protestant' denomination. One respondent expressed their understanding of what cultural-Catholicism means in a political or sectarian context in the following quotation:

> I think it's much more to do with cultural tribalism than it has to do with actual faith. I actually don't think it's a faith thing at all … a typical example of it is the Celtic Rangers thing. You see it so … and it's very obvious how you know the tribalism of Catholicism and you talk to people. If you look at Republicanism in the south of Ireland it has no affinity with Catholicism now, but if you look at [it] in the north they are so intertwined you know and they've become one and the same thing in one sense you know in parts, but it's much more a tribal thing.

Another respondent reflecting on the sectarian nature of religious identity in Northern Ireland commented that:

> In our Meeting we have quite a few people who are ex-Catholics who are now part of our Meeting. It's becoming easier for people to change from one denomination to another. At one time it could have been seen by many people as betraying your community to attend a Church of another denomination … I think that is much less so now – particularly in the south of Ireland.

My study also shows that culturally-Catholic respondents had to contend with other people's perceptions of Quakerism as an essentially British institution and this caused them to feel uncomfortable about this aspect of their chosen identity, as the following quotation illustrates:

> … but by and large they are seen as British especially by the Irish speaking public … I was talking about some of the things we are talking about now and I talked about my own membership of the Quakers … and the reasons I had gone in. I was saying that I felt that there was no future for the Vatican – that its power was contrary to the Gospel – and at the end a lady said to me … 'there isn't a future for the Quakers here' she said 'they're British' and because I wasn't expecting the remark and I wasn't ready for it and I did not know what to say … So I think I just stayed quiet and said nothing. But she was telling me that I had joined a British group.

However, as this respondent went on to say, the experience of mixing with Quakers from a different background had enabled her to rethink negative perceptions about Britishness:

> I can now talk to them and it has been a wonderful experience for me learning about Britishness and realising that Britishness carries huge integrity with it because I was brought up in school to think that the British were bad.

Findings about respondents who are cultural-Catholic are also very significant in the context of identity category change which Todd found was fairly unusual. These respondents had taken on a new religious identity and retained symbolic aspects of their previous identity – there was some dissonance between the two aspects of their identity which had to be managed by them.

Respondents who were not culturally-Catholic or were originally from non-Irish backgrounds talked about feeling like 'outsiders' at times for a number of reasons. For example, some respondents referred to Catholic 'sectarianism' in the Republic of Ireland, giving the example of the Ne Temere decree of 1908[33] which operated in both of the Irish states. According to the respondents this had a major impact on Catholic/Protestant relations, was very divisive and contributed to separate development of the communities, as the following quotations show with reference to the Republic of Ireland:

> When I came back from England in 1969 I joined the local Church of Ireland table tennis club and Roman Catholics weren't allowed to be members at that stage. Even if there was an interchurch couple the Catholic partner wasn't allowed to be a member and this was to do with the rules and regulations, because the Church of Ireland said that if you are going to play it that way we'll play it this way and so interchurch marriages weren't encouraged between Protestant and Catholics in that way.

> … and of course nobody went to each other's Churches. Nobody went to each other's funerals. I don't think they even went into each other's houses and part of it, a large part of it I think, even when I was a teenager, was the Ne Temere decree.

One respondent reflected on the sense that her 'Irishness' had to be substantiated:

> But there's always a question – and this is the sort of sectarianism of Catholics – if you are really Irish if you're not Catholic? If you're Catholic you don't really have to do anything. If you're Protestant you have to prove yourself by speaking Irish or becoming a member of a group that is overtly Irish nationalist otherwise you are still asked questions.

However, another respondent felt that Irish identity has become more inclusive:

> I think the non-Catholic population are possibly feeling more Irish. I mean we used to be regarded and to some extent regard ourselves as

---

33 This papal decree meant that before permission could be granted to a Catholic wanting to marry a non-Catholic in a religious wedding, the non-Catholic partner had to give an undertaking that any children born to the couple would be raised as Catholics (Mitchell 2006, 16).

> being what we call west Brits and I think that is gone for a number of reasons ... The president Mary McAleese[34] was very popular and very skilful and I think quite a lot was due to her.

The Irish language was very important to some respondents (especially those not originally from Ireland) – partly as a way of feeling part of the 'nation' but they also saw themselves as challenging the way that Irish Nationalism had claimed the language and culture as belonging to the Gaelic, that is Catholic, people, when it was originally much more non-sectarian and inclusive.

One respondent expressed her deep frustration that the Irish language was only taught at Catholic schools:

> Look I'm a Quaker, why should I have to send my daughter to a Catholic school, a school that's under Catholic patronage when we're not Catholic? We just want an Irish speaking school and the patronage should be open to all denominations. And the reaction from Catholics was 'well if you get enough Protestants together you can have your own.' Well I don't want my own. I want everybody to be together. I want inter-denominational education and that's one thing about Quaker schools is that they are open to all dominations.[35]

Another respondent in Northern Ireland talked about the difficulty of integrating different aspects of her identity (especially political ones) within Quakerism which relates to how 'symbolic distinctions' also operate within IYM. She mentioned that her need for political and social activism was drawn from elsewhere and Meeting for Worship was important for her spiritual journey; but more recently this has changed because there is a greater focus in Irish Quakerism now on issues such as environmentalism and economic injustice.

The next section develops the theme of sectarianism and respondents' experiences during the 'Troubles'.

4.4 *Reflections about the 'Troubles'*

Many respondents had very vivid memories of the 'Troubles'. Below is a selection of quotations from the interviews that illustrate both the impact on respondents' everyday lives and their understanding of the conflict.

---

34 The President of the Republic of Ireland from 1997–2011.

35 However some of the respondents do not approve of Quaker schools because they charge fees and this does not accord with their values.

I've got very strong memories of Bloody Sunday.[36] I can still remember sitting around the radio hearing the impact of that. The school was right in the centre of Belfast … The teachers saying that within a hundred yards of the school, 300 bombs had gone off. And I suppose as a child, as a young person, you know, it was very normal to have bombs going off all around the place. And there was trouble … it must have been terrible for my parents … life was very curtailed as a teenager. You could not go out to social activities. It was very much, had to be curtailed a lot and I think that was, you know, a great pity … I was very conscious of the 'Troubles'. I was very interested in history and politics. I was very interested in the situation. But you know, I was very fortunate, I wasn't personally impacted … but undoubtedly it was the big issue of life.

… you did not mix that way and I suppose I feel very angry about that. I think it's … the role of the state to give children opportunities to mix. It's a moral duty of all Churches to make sure that they [do] and that requires them to integrate schools and that was where life was. You know it was just the nature of where we were. Northern Ireland was very denominational at that time.

I come from a working class background and I grew up on the Shankill Road which was the heartland of kind of Protestantism so I'm very much aware of it. I was fortunate in that my parents were determined that both my brother and I would have a grammar school education. So that really helped us to kind of I suppose move on in areas that perhaps other people in the street that I lived did not have the opportunity to do. But in a sense why I'm saying it is because I feel I have an understanding of some of the behaviour and the responses and the way people have reacted to situations partly because of that.

I was 18 years of age that year and I was a member of the Girl Guides and my bus was stoned and I had kids on holiday in Newcastle and our bus

36 The events of 30 January 1972, known as 'Bloody Sunday', when British soldiers shot dead 13 people taking part in a banned civil rights march in Derry – the final death toll reached 14 when another casualty died of his wounds four months later (McKittrick and McVea 2001, 76–77). Military commanders later said that their troops had been shot at first. According to McKittrick and McVea, one of the main consequences of 'Bloody Sunday', and the Widgery Inquiry exonerating the British army, was an increase in Catholics joining republican paramilitary groups such as the IRA. Anglo-Irish relations were damaged and nationalists on both sides of the border took to the streets to protest (2001, 76–77).

> was the first bus to be stoned … the year was 1969… I think it might have been the 10th of July. We had been up there for the month of July with the kids and we were coming home on the 10th of July and the bus was stoned … It was years before I went across the border again.

The next quotation is from a respondent recounting her experiences of visiting Northern Ireland during the 'Troubles' and her observation about how things have changed since the political settlement.

> We were stopped at crossing points which they'd stop every so often and somebody warned us never to run away from, if you got to them and you turned around and ran away they'd shoot. I don't know if that's true or not, but we would wait and as soon as we spoke they just passed you without asking anything more, it was acceptable. One thing I did notice was that these soldiers were incredibly young and frightened to death. We'd be walking along the road and one of them would suddenly put his gun up like this and in his face was fear. And I thought I could quite see him shooting people by accident because he was so frightened … but since then going back there on a holiday with my daughter and we found it lovely, no borders, no police, no checkpoints – you crossed the border without knowing you'd crossed the border.

Attendance at Meeting for Worship for some Friends in Northern Ireland was at times a challenging experience during the 'Troubles'. This quotation, from a respondent from the Republic of Ireland who was visiting Bessbrook Quaker Meeting, neatly summarises both the unusual situation of Quakers holding a 'silent' Meeting for Worship and the difficulty non-Quakers had in identifying where Quakers 'fit' in terms of the sectarian divide:

> I remember going to Bessbrook again – having to pass through checkpoints to go to Meeting for Worship and then we were in the Meeting for Worship which would normally be silent and there were these helicopters low overhead – the presence of the English army was there continuously. One of the Quakers said, 'oh you don't have to take any notice of them. They're protecting us.' And another person said at that time that she did not know if the local people liked Quakers because they could not make up their mind what side they were on.

In terms of the theme raised in the previous quotation about Quakers and 'what side they were on', it was clear that Irish Quakers were faced with issues concerning religion, national identity and political affiliation and some of them identified with Nationalism and others with Unionism. However, I found that a number of Quakers sought to downplay the 'Protestant' roots of Quakerism in order to navigate a middle path between Catholic and Protestant sectarianism, and the respondents that I interviewed showed little evidence of 'oppositional' or 'thick' identities. The following quotation from a respondent reflecting on a question that his children asked about their religious identity, encapsulates this finding:

> I remember when we came back from (name of country) and they went to the Friends school, that inevitable thing when they came back after the first week and they asked are we Protestants or are we Catholics? Well we explained that they actually were Quakers.[37]

I now focus on what having a Quaker identity represents for two of the respondents: 'Peter' who lives in Northern Ireland and 'Sean' in the Republic of Ireland. (All the names in these case studies have been changed to preserve the anonymity of the respondents). I give examples of the way in which these respondents challenged their own sectarianism and sectarianism in the wider community. I contrast Peter and Sean's narratives and look at what they have in common in terms of their Quaker identity.

4.5 *Case Studies*

4.5.1 Peter

Peter is a 'birthright', evangelical[38] Quaker in Northern Ireland and lives and works in a predominantly unionist area. Peter explained that his parents would have considered themselves to be Protestant at the start of the 'Troubles'. Peter said about the tradition of Quakerism he grew up in:

> ... the key thing was up to that point I'd say in my life if you talk about Ulster Quakerism, you're talking about a tradition that certainly until during my teenage years was quite conservative, and I think in many ways very traditional and it's quite interesting that, and we'll get on to this

37 In a Quaker school of about 1200 students only 5 or 6 were Quakers, (interview with an Irish Quaker in 2011).

38 Bebbington's (1989) definition of evangelicalism consists of four elements: acceptance of conversion, belief in the Bible as the word of God, salvation is achieved through the death of Jesus Christ and faith is expressed through social action/ promoting the Christian message (Ganiel and Dixon 2008, 422). This definition fits Peter's religiosity in most aspects although his focus eventually changed from proselytising to social activism.

> when we talk about the Troubles, but a lot of the social activity initially among Friends in Ulster was driven by Friends in the Belfast area, and the more evangelical tradition at this end of the country was more interested in the issues of spiritual concerns … I grew up on that tradition where being saved was a really important part of who you were.

Marianne Elliott contends that it is very difficult for people in Northern Ireland to 'opt out' of sectarianism because of the way that it shapes people's identity (2009, 16). However, Peter gave many instances of how he challenged sectarianism from an early age, supported by his parents, who he said had different attitudes than other Protestant parents. For example, Peter decided to become a Celtic football supporter when he was seven although all his friends at school were supporters of Glasgow Rangers.[39] By the time he was eighteen Peter favoured the policies of the Social Democratic Labour Party (SDLP), 'which is a bit radical for somebody in a Protestant school' despite most of his friends supporting one of the Unionist parties. In a Northern Ireland Life and Times Survey conducted in 2003 it was found that only 2 percent of Protestants supported the SDLP (Mitchell 2006, 30–31), so Peter was very unusual in his choice of political party. Peter also had definite views about his nationality:

> I have a British passport because it's cheaper than the Irish one quite frankly no other good reason … I remember by the time I'm 16, 17, 18 being asked what's your nationality and I would write British stroke Irish. It was never British alone by that stage. I was already saying to myself well actually I have two identities here and they're both important to me and I don't want to deny either of them. They matter to me. They're part of who I am and so I was making statements to myself and being aware … at that stage as well I was also saying to myself well actually what matters is whether people are fairly treated and what about the kids who grew up on the Falls or the Shankill? Not that I knew them but I was aware that their lives were a lot worse than mine.

39 In Northern Ireland and Scotland, football is one of the ways that sectarianism and social identity is expressed. Two prominent Scottish football teams, Celtic and Glasgow Rangers, are strongly associated with the two communities in Northern Ireland, Celtic with Nationalism/Republicanism and Glasgow Rangers with Unionism/Loyalism. Rivalry between the teams is intense, not only in sporting terms, but because they represent the two communities in conflict with each other during the 'Troubles' (Burdsey and Chappell 2003, 7). Peter, as a young Quaker in a Protestant school, chose to consciously support a team that represented the 'other' tradition marking him out as different from his peers.

Peter was conscious of the 'Troubles' during his childhood and the potential to be caught up in dangerous situations. He said that he was not personally affected by the conflict due to his protective family and the specific geographical locality where the violence mainly occurred. Peter talked about how he became increasing aware during his secondary school years of injustice in Northern Ireland and realised that injustice bothered him. These examples of choices Peter made as a young man shows his awareness of sectarianism and how he was prepared to risk alienation from his peer group to make his own decisions. In talking about his motivation for the decisions he made Peter said that:

> I'm someone who's driven by the idea that you choose things by principles and by values and by … and also by experience. In other words if I've had a living relationship with the inward Christ how am I going to deny that?

After his return from university Peter joined the family business and said he was determined to increase the number of Catholics in his workforce. This was very difficult because the business was in a Protestant area of the town. In 1993 many commercial buildings, including Peter's, were blown up by a paramilitary bomb. The annual Loyalist parade from Drumcree Church was the source of much sectarian violence in the area at the time.[40] Peter talked about the violence in the streets of Portadown during the period leading up to the parade and about going out with his father to separate people from the different communities who were fighting each other. It was also very common for Catholic employees to be ostracised by Protestant colleagues in the build-up to the 12th of July. Peter was determined that this would not happen in his workplace. However, his efforts to create a non-sectarian atmosphere were undermined by his manager 'Neil', a unionist and member of the Orange Order. Peter said:

> I remember the first 4 or 5 years … because he [Neil] used to put bunting outside our factory kind of without asking me and he put this Protestant bunting up and I said I don't want Protestant bunting up because all that says to the Catholic employees that I have you know you're not welcome.

40 In 1995 a decision was made by senior police offers to change the parade route. This led to the 'Drumcree stand-off' when members of the Orange Order sought to follow their long established route which passed by a mainly nationalist housing estate on the Garvaghy road. Katy Radford suggests that this situation led to a highly charged atmosphere, and violence. There was also criticism of the authorities in the way they responded to the communities' competing demands (2004, 138).

> I'm supporting this thing and I'm not even supporting it. So it was a bit of a nightmare. And I remember going to Neil and Neil saying don't touch it because if you do you'll have the town, the local Protestant community after you. He had enough insight into how the Protestant community worked that he was wise enough to say, he was sympathetic. By this stage he was beginning to understand even though he did not agree with me, he understood where I stood and was trying to say 'Peter just cool your horses, look I'm just, I know you've got good reason to be annoyed about this because they had no right to get up on your building and attach bunting' because they had climbed up on my roof and done all this.
>
> So over the years we got the message through to the street that I actually, the only thing the least they could do was ask us, and in the end as time has gone by they've actually come each year and I'll say to them 'I'm not happy but I don't really have any choice, do I?' And they'll say 'no, we would really like to do it …' It's very interesting the last 2 or 3 years; the bunting hasn't gone up on the street. The place is moderating.

Elliott describes the displays on occasions such as the 12th of July as an example of cultural defensiveness common to Protestants and Catholics in Northern Ireland, adding that people who have a secure identity are less likely to feel the need to defend it (2009, 8). In his opposition to the bunting Peter was challenging the cultural norms of the wider Protestant community. Peter took this even further by rejecting Protestantism as a personal category in certain situations. He told me that when completing the form monitoring the 'community background' of his workforce, introduced as part of the Fair Employment and Treatment (Northern Ireland) Order 1998, he put himself down as 'other' rather than ticking the Catholic or Protestant box.[41]

Peter was able to maintain his stance about the bunting over a period of years, despite the risk of alienation from the local Protestant community. How difficult this is was confirmed by another respondent:

> … you'd have to have grown up in Northern Ireland particularly with a religious background to know how difficult it is to step outside the parameters of your belief systems that in doing so there is partly the guilt thing that trips in at some degree there is approval or disapproval kicks in as well.

41 This measure was introduced to tackle discrimination on the grounds of religious beliefs or political affiliation in employment, education and the provision of goods and services (Equality Commission for Northern Ireland: ECNI).

The same person also acknowledged the pervasive influence of sectarianism even in people who are self-aware and committed to challenging negative stereotypes:

> I'm going to make two contradictory statements. I don't believe I'm sectarian but I believe we're all sectarian. You cannot grow up in Northern Ireland without – because it's been imbued in you as part of your whole upbringing so you have to keep watching out for it all the time.

However, Peter seemed to feel a very strong sense of belonging to his Quaker evangelical Meeting and this connection may have acted as a protective factor against social isolation.[42]

4.5.2 Sean

I now contrast the experiences of Peter with Sean, who is a Quaker from a Roman Catholic background in the Republic of Ireland. Sean said about his memories of Ireland as a young man:

> So growing up in Ireland in the 50s it was quite a fundamentalist place in terms of Catholicism and we did not know it. You see that was the scary bit … So because we did not know Protestants, we held an identity which was separate and that separate identity, all that was left of it eventually was Catholicism because the Irish language went. So out of that powerlessness there came our separate identity in Catholicism and we took all the glory of that and looked down on the Prods you know … I thought Paisley was nuts but I can see our part in winding him up. Triumphalism, the triumphalism of Catholicism, our dead-sureness of stuff and of course I think the younger people, I don't know about today, but certainly I took it very seriously.

Sean's account supports Elliott's view that negative stereotyping has been a feature of relations between people throughout the island of Ireland, not just in Northern Ireland (2009, 6). Furthermore, Elliott argues that the way Irishness came to be associated with Catholicism, with an identity formed from the experience of destitution and colonialism, led to a narrow definition of who could belong to the Irish nation (2009, 8). This is compounded by the way that

42 Samuel Stroope argues that people with traditional religious beliefs tend to feel a strong sense of belonging to their faith group because there is a shared belief system (2011, 571–572).

Catholic and Protestant young people in both parts of Ireland grow up learning different 'versions' of Irish history in school (Elliott 2009, 10).

Sean talked about his disenchantment with Catholicism and exploring the Charismatic Renewal movement[43] before eventually coming to Quakerism in the 1970s. Sean described himself as having come out of the Green (Irish nationalist) tradition and how he was affected by the outbreak of the 'Troubles' and in particular the events of 'Bloody Sunday' – the significance of which was explained in section 4. Sean felt at home with the close-knit community at his Quaker Meeting and the pacifist position of Quakerism strongly appealed to him. However, this comfortable feeling was disturbed by an experience Sean had one Sunday when he attended a Meeting for Worship:

> I remember the shock coming in here on a November morning and 'John' and 'Margaret' (two long-standing Quakers) were wearing poppies. The shock of it ... they were red and it was a red rag to a bull coming out of the Green tradition. I mean I had known two men who had fought at Kilmichael[44] and one of them had a big garden and when poppies came up he'd run down and pull them up you know. That's how I grew up a child. Poppies represented comfort for the British army and going into Meeting and seeing 4 or 5 people with poppies was a shock. What the fuck was I doing here? And a part of me kind of I think just widening my perspective.

Sean had already developed a warm relationship with the two Quakers wearing the poppies and referred to them as being significant role models for him. Being part of a Quaker community with an emphasis on connection, so that very different points of view can be held within the Meeting, enabled Sean see other perspectives:

43 Charismatic Renewal (CR) is a Pentecostal movement which started in the US in the 1950s and by the 1970s became very popular among Catholics in Ireland. Research by Mitchell and Ganiel indicates that some evangelical Protestant Christians moved towards a 'theology of inclusion' after sharing spiritual experiences with Catholics in the CR movement (2011, 128). A number of respondents had taken part in CR services and stated that the movement was popular with a range of Christians seeking a more emotionally expressive form of spirituality.

44 This refers to an attack by the West Cork IRA on an auxiliary police unit in 1920 which resulted in several police deaths and was regarded by republicans as a great victory over the British forces (Moloney 2007, 176).

> I liked the conversations I had with 'John' and 'Margaret'. They were never that extensive but they were here and so I kind of could not dismiss them, so I had to learn to calm down and try and understand it.[45]

This shows that Sean was able to recognise his own sectarian attitudes and stand back from them. In addition, Sean went beyond just understanding the diversity of Irish Quakerism to be able to take into account very different perspectives of other Quakers more vocal than John and Margaret. For example, Sean described his experience of attending a Yearly Meeting and hearing the views of a Northern Irish Quaker about a politician in the Republic of Ireland:

> I remember up at a Yearly Meeting in Belfast at breakfast one morning and Peter Barry[46] was foreign minister at the time … I mean a more innocuous man you could not meet … I was sitting at breakfast one morning and there was someone at the other side of the table like calling Peter Barry an IRA supporter. So again I had to bring myself to try and understand both sides, my own and the others'.

Sean summarised his approach in the following way:

> So I think that the nature of living in the world we have to say right and wrong about things – but if we're to understand the dynamics, if we're to bring healing to hurt you have to take that peculiar place in the middle which says let's just understand it, let's soothe ourselves in the awfulness, learn to tolerate the awfulness, so we can understand the dynamics of history and hurt. So it's about learning to tolerate the awfulness, to come out of reactivity – basically a spiritual kind of idea – letting go of idealism.

I asked Sean if he now sees himself as a Protestant and he laughed out loud saying:

---

45 Douglas Davies describes how people joining a new group tend to adapt themselves to fit in with prevailing norms, seeking out insiders to act as role models to help with this process (2008, 12). It is significant that Sean mentions that the conversations were not that extensive which implies that John and Margaret themselves were minimising or avoiding contentious issues that could have created tension in their Quaker community.

46 Peter Barry was the Minister for Foreign Affairs in the Dáil Éireann between 1982 and 1987. He helped to negotiate the 1985 Anglo-Irish Agreement which was extremely unpopular with many unionists (Coogan 1995, 197).

> … I know I have to have labels for certain situations but essentially I see myself as just a human being who I can certainly say Irish by culture, Catholic by culture. By practice I'm happier here with Quakers.

Sean demonstrated an ability to transcend aspects of his cultural identity and to acknowledge the different identities of other Quakers by 'taking the peculiar place in the middle', which is an aspect of identity not specifically explored in Todd's work. However, Sean's very clear statement about his identity being Irish and Catholic by culture, although he is content to call himself a Quaker, confirms Todd's conclusions about the potency of certain aspects of personal identity in Ireland. What is novel about my findings is the particular 'hybrid' identity of respondents, such as Sean, who manage to encompass a Quaker identity within their cultural-Catholicism. Tom Inglis refers to cultural barriers that make it problematic for people to leave Catholicism for another Christian denomination due to the negative associations of Protestantism with colonialism (2007, 212). Inglis proposes a typology of Catholics which includes a definition of cultural Catholicism which is different than the one suggested by my respondents. Inglis asserts that although the identification of cultural Catholics is more with the heritage of the Church than the institution, they still regard themselves as Catholic and would not consider finding another religious affiliation (2007, 215). According to Inglis:

> Being Catholic is like some indelible mark that they have accepted and have no desire to change. It is literally part of what they are, in the same way that they are, for example, white, male, and Irish. (2007, 215–6)

However, as I have outlined in this paper, this barrier has largely been overcome by Quakers from a Catholic background who have found it possible to retain their cultural identity and belong to another Christian group.[47]

Mitchell's contention that some aspects of identity may be accentuated by circumstances or the behaviour of other people is seen in the example of Sean, who became very conscious of his Irish nationalist roots when he saw the red poppies worn by fellow Quakers to commemorate Remembrance Day. This also works in the way that we are perceived by other people, for example, Peter

---

47 I have no data about the number of people in Ireland who are culturally-Catholic and transfer to another religious affiliation. My sense is that it is not very common. For example, in my large, extended Irish Catholic family I appear to be the only one who has done this.

having his factory covered in unionist bunting because in that situation he was regarded as being part of the Protestant community. As Mitchell suggests the concept of community is also based on social categorisations – it is not something that is fixed, and exists in the perceptions of people who feel part of a specific community and also those who observe and describe that community (2006, 12–13).

Peter and Sean appear to represent two very different strands of Irish Quakerism. Peter is from an evangelical, Protestant background in a unionist area of Northern Ireland. Sean grew up in an Irish post-colonial society that was shaped by the central role of the Roman Catholic Church. However, I suggest that Peter and Sean have more in common than may be initially apparent. For example, both men sought to challenge sectarianism in their part of Ireland. They actively transcended aspects of their social identity, for example, in Peter's case his choice of political affiliation and hybrid national identity, and the way he responded to sectarian attitudes and behaviour in his own community and workplace. Peter also modified his evangelicalism considerably in order to act as a bridge between evangelical and liberal Friends. Sean's approach reflected the reality of living in a part of Ireland not directly affected by the 'Troubles'. He demonstrated a willingness to encompass the perspective of Quakers from a traditional 'Protestant' background and examine attitudes formed by his cultural heritage. However, he retained a strong attachment to his Catholic background as one aspect of a multi-faceted identity.

To conclude, these two case studies illustrate my finding that these respondents have a form of 'hybrid' identity that is much more flexible and reflexive than was found in Todd's study, and their accounts demonstrate evidence of identity fluidity and change.

4.6 *The Culture of Irish Quakerism*

This section moves from a discussion of the identity of individual Friends to the culture of the Quaker organisation in Ireland. The interplay between individuals and organisational culture is a key theme. I argue that the culture of Irish Quakerism has both adapted to individual members, for example, through the influence of culturally-Catholic Friends joining the Society, and that in turn the culture of Quakerism has impacted on individuals' sense of identity.

Mats Alvesson asserts that 'a sense of common, taken for granted ideas, beliefs and meanings are necessary for continuing organized activity' – adding that this facilitates connections between people in the organisation and reduces confusion and constant reinterpretation of the meanings of key organisational goals (2002, 2). In defining what culture is, Alvesson suggests that it is ‘understood to be a system of common symbols and meanings’ (2002, 3) and goes on to add that culture is not something that exists mainly within individuals but takes place in the interactions between people ‘where symbols and meanings are publicly expressed’ (2002, 4). However, Martin Parker argues that although in general this definition of organisational culture is accurate his research suggests that organisations can also have ‘multiple divides’, related to specific ‘affiliations or schisms’ within the organisations (2000, 187). Parker suggests that ‘these divisions function as a way of classifying the identity of self and other, in effect, of grounding a particular assertion about the distinctiveness of an individual or group’ (2000, 188).

Section 1 provided an introduction to Quaker culture and highlighted a number of key aspects relevant for this study. For example, adherents assert that all can have a direct relationship with God – and are guided by the principle of ‘the priesthood of all believers’. This means that sharing responsibility for the function and structure of the organisation is a fundamental aspect of Quaker theology and all roles within the organisation rotate and are decided by a process of discernment. In addition, discernment is the basis for decision making through the Quaker business method where, as Dandelion argued, ‘they claim to ‘discern’ the will of God’ (2008b, 52–53). Because of the diverse culture of Quakerism in Ireland it can be argued this has posed particular challenges in terms of Alvesson’s reference to ‘common, taken for granted ideas, beliefs and meanings.’ Examples of these challenges are explored in this section. The next section discusses some of the different forms of identity that make up the culture of IYM.

4.7 *Political Identity and Affiliation*

Some respondents felt that Friends in Northern Ireland tend to avoid involvement in party politics for a number of reasons, as illustrated by the following quotation:

> On the whole Friends tend not to be party political – they will campaign in peace movements, in movements for social justice – at the same time there is always a worry ‘oh should we be in with this group because they might be members of Sinn Féin’. There is a fear of contamination by groups who have a tradition of violence and being identified, among some Friends – not all. Not all have that fear.

The issue of ‘contamination’ will be explored more fully when I look at how the Yearly Meeting responded as a corporate body to the ‘Troubles’. However, my findings showed that there were different perspectives about the involvement of Friends in certain aspects of political activism, as the following quotation illustrates:

> It's true to say that we have within this Quarterly Meeting everything from Sinn Féin through to the Democratic Unionist Party [DUP] and that reality is a very interesting one. You've got this mad diversity of political as well as theological [affiliations] and it's usually, that you can be pretty sure, that the evangelicals will be DUP – although that's not by any means ... but there's one or two would be on the liberal wing of Quakerism so you have a spectrum in both within Ulster Meeting. And you have members who are members of the Orange Order ... And we have had Minutes – Minutes from Quarterly Meeting saying Friends should be discouraged from joining the Orange Order ... In the end I think they began to see ... that actually it wasn't a very Christian thing to be doing at all. They perceived it to be part of their Christian life, because that's the way the Orange Order is presented to a lot of people.

As well as describing the diverse political affiliations of Quakers in Northern Ireland this quotation also highlights the connection between political and theological outlook and, in particular, observations in the Quaker identity matrix 4.5, about the evangelical Friends who were embedded in their unionist communities.

A number of respondents in the Republic of Ireland felt very strongly that religious groups should remain apart from party politics because of negative associations with the influential role of the Roman Catholic Church, as the following quotation illustrates:

> It's left to individual Friends who are working in various organisations to try to come up with a Friendly line on various things. I don't think there'd be enough agreement across the political spectrum within Friends to be able to come up with a cohesive statement. I think it's inevitable, and I would be unhappy if it was to happen, because it would be kind of like the model of the Roman Church attempting to control the state in Ireland ... and I think the idea of a religious community becoming a force in politics is a recipe for disaster.

However, some Friends did volunteer their political affiliations and a number were active within some of the smaller political parties in the Republic of Ireland, for example, the Green Party and the Progressive Democrats were specifically mentioned. In Northern Ireland some Friends supported non-sectarian groups such as the Alliance party or a mainstream nationalist party like the SDLP; this can be seen as being linked to the 'Quaker not Protestant' position of Friends explored in this part of the monograph.

4.8 *Cultural-Catholicism*

Section 1 highlighted the significance of Friends joining the Society from Catholic and other Christian backgrounds and the impact of this on the culture of Irish Quakerism, in the sense that it contributed towards IYM having a number of equally strong identities. In this section I specifically discuss cultural-Catholicism and why there might have been some difficulty welcoming people from a Catholic background to Quakerism. One explanation was given by Quaker House representatives, Janet and Alan Quilley, who observed that:

> Janet Quilley: one of the first things that really did I could not get my head round at Yearly Meeting ... was about burials in Quaker graveyards and this was such an issue as to whether people who were not Quakers could be buried there, and it wasn't till a little way down the line that I understood why this was so important, because in the south it was very very likely that people had come from a Catholic background and may well be married to a Catholic and when they got buried they'd like their spouse to be there too ...
>
> Alan Quilley: ... which might mean a priest coming along.
>
> Janet Quilley: and it really took me some time to get my head round why it was so important, and why yes they could do that and why people in the north could not accept that.

Other observations were to do with the reasons why people give up their previous religious affiliation and how this might impact on the Society. On respondent said:

> We've had this great influx of people from Catholicism and from other backgrounds so the nature of the Society has changed because these people bring their life experience – a certain amount of baggage with them.

Other respondents were concerned about how Friends by 'convincement' learnt about Quaker culture and adapted to it. They observed that some Friends' rejection of the hierarchy of Roman Catholicism had attracted them to the more egalitarian structures and practices of Quakerism but eventually became impatient with how these processes worked. Another respondent stated that:

> When I was growing up we absorbed a great deal through the pores so to speak, as 'birthright' Friends, because we were growing up in a Quaker household, and we would have grace before meals and we understood that, this was our understanding of when Jesus said 'do this in memory of me'. Other people grew up and had the Eucharist and the bread and the wine. We have a period of quiet reflection and give thanks before meals. People coming in from outside haven't sat through Monthly Meeting and Yearly Meeting for years ... so therefore haven't absorbed a lot of the things. We learnt a lot 'sitting by Nelly', so to speak, which we need to teach other people, so they have an understanding, because other than that it only takes one clerk who doesn't understand and doesn't do things the way they ought to be done and the memory's gone. We're at a point now where we are starting to have clerks' training courses. It's very necessary because there is the knowledge and the approach to business that we need to be able to share.

At the Yearly Meeting I attended in 2011, a special interest group called 'RC to Q' (Roman Catholicism to Quakerism) focused on what former Catholics bring to Quakerism, the perceptions of other Quakers and how this could 'help or hinder the development' of Irish Quakerism (Minihan 2011, 4). A further workshop was added to the programme because of the popularity of this event. At the second session a participant mentioned that in Northern Ireland very few Catholics moved to Quakerism and some that did had not received a warm welcome. This observation highlights one of Jennifer Todd's findings, about the awareness of religious distinctions in Northern Ireland. At the end of the workshop a strong commitment was expressed by Friends present to take this discussion forward, both in terms of helping to integrate newer Quakers from a Catholic background and the Society adjusting to this development (field notes, IYM, Dublin 2011).

Peter Macallister, a Friend from Northern Ireland, describes himself as growing up in a nationalist area of West Belfast during the 'Troubles', leaving the Catholic Church and moving to England after 'having had enough of the violent sectarian bigotry' in Northern Ireland and becoming a 'convinced' Friend (2011, 12). Macallister said that:

> When the IRA cease fire came into effect I returned to Northern Ireland full of optimism and buoyed up by the deep influence of English

> Quakerism and early Friends had on me. I felt this form of Quakerism so uplifting and alive compared to the toxic sectarian nature of much of Northern Ireland Protestantism and Catholicism. For me Quakerism stood apart and above these forms of Christianity.... (2011, 12)

Macallister goes on to describe how some Friends in Northern Ireland responded when he shared his experiences of English Quakerism by saying 'that English and Irish Quakerism were not the same.' As Macallister acknowledged: 'This is of course true as Friends in Ireland, and Northern Ireland particularly, have been affected by the political, social, historical, sectarian and religious influences of the partitioned island' (2011, 12). Macallister added that he did not recognise much of what he saw in Northern Ireland as Quakerism as he understood it, and commented on the evangelical and unionist outlook of Friends in the rural areas of Northern Ireland compared to the more diverse form in the urban areas. However, following his attendance at the 'RC to Q' workshop Macallister hopes that 'Meetings in Northern Ireland might one day feel more able to explore the positive aspects of Catholicism and the values that are shared with Quakerism' (2011, 12).

The Yearly Meeting in 2012 had a follow up to the 'RC to Q' workshop with a special interest group called 'Liberal Irish Quakers – weighty Friends or supermarket Christians?' (Culturally-Catholic Friends are predominantly liberal). This session was advertised as an exploration and discussion of 'liberal Quaker stereotypes.' This was also a well-attended workshop and I observed some very thoughtful, deep and respectful discussion between participants (field notes, IYM, Dublin 2012). The interest groups referred to above are indicative of the overlap between the cultural and theological identity of Friends within Irish Quakerism which is explored in the next section.

4.9 *Theological Identity*

As previously mentioned, the Religious Society of Friends in Ireland includes both evangelical and liberal Quakers. The majority of evangelical Quakers are in Northern Ireland and many are also part of an evangelical Protestant and unionist subculture. There are also a number of liberal Friends – many based in the urban areas of Northern Ireland. The Republic of Ireland is predominantly liberal with a minority of evangelical Friends. The basis of this theological spectrum which is unique in worldwide Quakerism was explored in section 2, and it also relates to the different political and social cultures of the two Irish states. This quotation from a respondent encapsulates the theological spectrum of Irish Quakerism:

> Dublin is probably quite a good reflection of overall Irish Quakerism in that we have great extremes of theological outlook. We have people who are virtually agnostic down to people who are very dependent on the Bible, very clear that Christ was both fully divine and fully human and that his death on the cross was very significant and that he rose from the dead. The number of, if you want to use the label evangelical Friends in Dublin, is now very small and I think sometimes I personally feel a siege mentality but on the other hand I appreciate so much the friendship … with [people] whom I would differ hugely – makes me value the fact that we can live together within the Society.

In my research I found that this diversity of theological outlook was the source of some tension within the Society. This is reflected in the outlook of a number of liberal Friends who talked about feeling more comfortable with the non-theistic language used by some Quakers in Britain Yearly Meeting. For example, this respondent explained what Quakerism meant to them:

> I'm getting back to what the essence of Quakerism is. It's based on testimonies. We don't have creeds we have testimonies. We live something out and we live out what our creed is.

This observation was borne out by my findings – liberal Friends did largely refer to their Quaker spirituality being expressed in social justice campaigns and other forms of activism. In contrast, evangelical Friends mainly talked about having a personal relationship with Jesus Christ; one respondent said:

> My relationship with Jesus Christ is undoubtedly real to me. I know that I believe absolutely … that Christ is there and dwells within me and has an impact on my life.

As Mitchell and Ganiel indicate, simplistic stereotypes of evangelical Christians in Northern Ireland do not match the diversity of belief, political affiliation and perspectives on social issues found in their research and other studies. They also point to the differences between evangelicals in terms of gender, social class and location in rural or urban areas (2011, 19). The same can be said for their counterparts in the Republic of Ireland. However, it is clear from my research that there is an aspect of the evangelical Quakerism that conforms with traditional evangelical Christianity, both theologically and in terms of attitudes to certain social issues. This is illustrated by the following extract from the website of Grange Friends Meeting, in County Tyrone, Northern Ireland:

> *Statement of Belief*
> Grange Preparative Meeting of the Religious Society of Friends adheres to the great foundation truths of Holy Scripture. We regard the whole Bible as the inspired Word of God and of final authority, and that there is no salvation, except through the atoning work of Christ, who is God manifested in the flesh and revealed to us by the Holy Spirit ... (Grange Friends Meeting).
>
> In contrast to the position taken by Grange PM, Friends from South Belfast PM express a distinctively more liberal tone regarding the values and theology of Quakerism. For example, the following are extracts from the beliefs section on their website:
>
> > *A Way To God* Quakers share a way of life rather than a set of beliefs. We seek to experience God directly, within ourselves and in our relationships with others and the world around us. These direct encounters with the Divine are where Quakers find meaning and purpose.
> > *Quakers and Christianity* The Quaker way has its roots in Christianity and finds inspiration in the Bible and the life and teachings of Jesus. Quakers also find meaning and value in other writings and in the teachings of other faiths and acknowledge that ours is not the only way.
> > *Working for a better world* Our religious experience leads us to place a special value on truth, equality, simplicity and peace. These testimonies, as they are known, are lived rather than written. They lead Quakers to translate their faith into action by working locally and globally for social justice, to support peacemakers and care for the environment (South Belfast Friends Meeting).

I found that for some evangelical Friends Quakerism was more like the outer form of their Christianity than the inner core, as this respondent explained:

> I regard Quakerism as a box, a wrapping for my Christian faith, and the reason the reasons I have remained a Friend are various one ... I think Quakerism at its best is the closest I've ever encountered to what I see as the experience of the early Church.

The following quotation is an evangelical perspective which challenges the emphasis on what they regard as the 'faith in action' or the social activism of some, mainly liberal, Friends:

> It's not that it [Quakerism] can supply the answers. I mean the answer is not a series of ideas. It's a relationship with Jesus Christ or with God through Jesus Christ ... so Quakerism could if it could get its act together and actually tell people what we're about and not about, peace and ecology and stuff, which are only to my mind applied religion.

However, some respondents were uncomfortable with religious labels and reflected that there was a tendency towards liberal 'fundamentalism'. One said that: 'I don't like the labels evangelical or liberal because I feel that we who call ourselves liberal have an evangelical cast.'

Elizabeth Duke's findings confirmed my observations about the theological diversity of Friends and also outlined some of the resulting tensions, as the following extract illustrates:

> The *diversity of belief* among Irish Friends could be seen either positively or negatively. Some Friends with a Christian commitment were seriously worried by the perceived dominance of non-Christians: 'If you have some Christian faith, you're becoming increasingly disenfranchised among Friends. We're missing the historical and spiritual core of Jesus.' Others felt that 'telling people they need salvation doesn't work; I need to reach out in love and tenderness ... We can't know the experiences of others'; 'I have felt the Holy Spirit in a kibbutz and in Muslim friends; you can't shut God in a box'. Similar differences were expressed by Friends who did not use Christian language. Negatively, 'I find some unease among Friends in Ireland about moving out of the box; I prefer the British *Quaker Faith and Practice* to the Ireland book ... I wouldn't have been attracted to some Meetings in Ireland'; 'a fundamentalist approach to the Bible that seems to me not to be part of a rich Quaker diversity, but could rather be the undoing of the Quaker dream'. In contrast, 'If their words lead them to their salvation, I am happy for them, so long as they don't want me to do it. We are on the same path at different angles.' 'I can appreciate how people for whom [salvation] has meaning have a Hallelujah feeling.' (Duke 2012b, 10)

This section outlined the diverse nature of the culture and identity of IYM. The following sections set out some of the challenges this diversity presents in maintaining the unity of the Society.

4.10 *Challenges to Unity*

4.10.1 The 'Troubles'

The diverse political and cultural backgrounds of Friends, particularly in Ulster QM, meant that the Yearly Meeting's response was mainly limited to agreement about the necessity to find a peaceful solution to the conflict in Northern Ireland. However, for some Friends this approach has been viewed as an avoidance of addressing the roots of the conflict, as seen in these comments:

> There's been a good number of Quaker projects in the north but we've been very reluctant to engage with things in a political way and very reluctant to call a wrong a wrong. I can't see any records of Quakers supporting the civil rights movement. I can't see any record of them saying that what brought about the civil rights movement was wrong.

Another respondent suggested that this had to do with the traditionally unionist culture of Irish Quakerism, particularly in Northern Ireland:

> If you're living in a rural area and you're trying to be live with your neighbours who are predominantly Protestant and unionist you're not going rock the boat with them and I think that was one of the issues. I think it's still one of the issues. The geographical and cultural background of Ulster Quakers is one that as a Yearly Meeting we're still trying to grapple with. It still spills out in a whole range of things. It spills out in the divisions in our Yearly Meeting all the time. The part of it, I've always felt, is got to do with much more about not wanting to let themselves down in front of their neighbours who are of that strong Protestant, Ulster Protestant tradition.

A common theme in the interviews was the concern expressed or observed by some respondents that talking openly with each other about issues that highlight major theological and political divisions in the Society would result in a schism, as this quotation illustrates:

> There's the very evangelical element in Quakers which would be very strident in their approach and there's the very liberal element in Quakers which would be almost too loose for some people. That's actually where you would see it and for long time ne'er the twain should meet, although it's getting better over time. What I have noticed is that if people don't agree they don't partake, so one of my biggest fears has been the possibility of a schism and I remember way back – we had the Yearly Meeting

> in Waterford one year, and I could see it rolling out in front of me, and it was actually over the peace process ... because it was very anti-IRA, very anti-republican, very anti-nationalist ... everyone was afraid to talk to one another. They were terrified of mentioning it ... I said to them you won't cause a schism if you talk, you'll cause a schism if you don't talk, because actually what happens is people leave ... So I would say to people you need to be able to agree to disagree.

One respondent's perspective was that in Northern Ireland some Quaker Meetings were inward looking, wanting to have a good relationship with everyone. They had no issue with civil rights, their attitude being 'we are living in a democracy so what's the problem?' This person observed that there was an issue with English Friends coming to Northern Ireland from a different social class compared to Ulster Quakers who were mainly from a rural background. English Quakers were seen as more intellectual, university educated, saying what needed to be done to address the conflict and creating organisations. Ulster Friends had no problem with services being provided – the problem was with the use of violence and republican aims for a United Ireland and the constitutional question (this point was reiterated by a number of respondents). Unionists (including Quakers) would have hardened their position (personal correspondence, 2012).

A number of respondents referred to the very difficult discussion and 'lack of unity' regarding an application for membership from an attender who was a member of Sinn Féin. Application for formal membership of the Religious Society of Friends is considered using the Quaker business method. According to Dandelion, 'Unity is considered as a sign of discerning God's will accurately, disunity as a sign that further work needs to be done ...' (2008b, 129). In effect, the outcome was that the application for membership in this case was neither denied nor granted because 'lack of unity' meant that a decision could not be made. Another application for membership can be made in the future if there is a change in circumstances, however, this applicant decided not to.

Apparently the applicant referred to above had a long history of involvement in peace making activities which included promoting a political settlement to the 'Troubles' within the republican movement. I was told that although some Friends supported this application there were others who felt very strongly that being a member of Sinn Féin was incompatible with the peace testimony. The other main objection came from Friends with a unionist background and may have indicated a sectarian basis linked to prejudicial views of Sinn Féin as an organisation. It was stressed that Friends, like all Churches in Northern Ireland, were and are a complicated mix of political views and backgrounds.

The 'lack of unity' about this application – which highlighted the different perspectives of Friends on this issue – was apparently so painful that even though it occurred many years ago it is still difficult for those concerned to discuss the situation openly.

One respondent talked about there being:

> A series of undercurrents in the north between the more liberal, whatever you mean by that, Friends maybe around South Belfast and the Friends more out west who, they didn't really want to have a block put between them and the other Protestants in their community. So they would have been a bit touchy about some of the contacts and you'd be frightened because you wouldn't want to put a step wrong and suddenly either let the side down or leave yourselves open to attack. A number of Friends had relatives who'd died in the Troubles. A number of Friends had their premises regularly bombed out and burned.

Some Friends managed the boundary between having a 'concern'[48] about the 'Troubles' and being part of a diverse religious community by acting on a more individual basis. One example is the work of Victor Bewley, a Dublin Quaker, who was asked by republican paramilitaries to act as a conduit to British government officials. As Rachel Bewley-Bateman commented, this had to be managed very carefully:

> Quaker procedure can be very long drawn out. If you want to do everything by committee it can take a little bit of time and some things are, it's better for the person with the concern to work with it … if I develop a concern I theoretically take it to my PM and with a bit of luck it might go on to Monthly Meeting and Quarterly Meeting and Yearly Meeting but how long does that take? And sometimes it's appropriate and sometimes the work is better done quietly by the person who has the concern … but obviously people can't do everything and in terms of off the record conversations, you can't have off the record conversations if too many people know about them anyway.

Another respondent gave examples of where they believed the Religious Society of Friends declined to position itself, identifying the partition of Ireland as the key point when the foundation of the new Northern Irish state created structural inequality for the nationalist minority:

48 Dandelion refers to a concern as '[a] 'leading' from God to action' (2008b, 130).

> I have not come across statements from Quakers supporting or saying that the state that evolved in Northern Ireland after the division was wrong and that the attempt by the unionists to hold on to their majority by gerrymandering was wrong. There are no statements either during the period or subsequent to the period. There is no sense that a wrong was done. Equally there is no very clear statement by Quakers saying that the campaign by the Provos[49] was wrong as well. We just don't do it, we don't stand up and say this is wrong ... we're not very good at saying that this is wrong. We try to get sides to talk. We try to alleviate distress. We try to alleviate the suffering. We're still not very good at saying 'this is wrong'.

Another respondent also asserted that the Religious Society of Friends failed to speak out about specific human rights violations during the Troubles:

> But taking on the hard human rights issues like Bloody Sunday, like the Birmingham Six, like the Guildford Four, like strip searching – anything like that. I feel that in some way open discussion on those issues has been or was silenced – we've been silent as a body and that's probably because it would be seen as taking sides – possibly would have been seen as taking up issues that were being struggled for by mainly people from the Catholic community or more specifically the republican community, that would be my understanding. I think there are two strands ... I think some of it is the concern about not taking sides and that it was important for Quakers to be able to be a 'bridge' in Northern Ireland and some of the reluctance could possibly be said to be sectarian. These would probably be the two main reasons why those issues have never been brought up – have never been corporately looked at.

The following quotation is an example of a respondent's opinion of how 'political' Irish Quakerism is in the sense of avoidance of sensitive subjects and the impact this has on communication between Friends:

> I think Irish Quakerism is very muted, silenced almost, almost in talking to each other we don't talk deeply to each other. We talk politically. I mean political in the [sense] we negotiate ... If I feel that you're an evangelical I will avoid any deep talk about religion ... and so, and then we all get on awfully well, much too well really.

49 Members of the Provisional IRA.

I asked if the differences are silencing people and the respondent replied:

> Yes, and I mean silence in all kinds of senses. Silence in the sense that we don't even deal with conflict. *We have silenced conflict itself.* Yet we talk about peace and we stand for peace and I don't think there can be any peace unless we are prepared to get into the fire ... we have to get into the conflict and try and understand it but that's what we don't, we don't even do. Issues like Irish politics we hardly get into them at all. I think we would be, are slow about entering that area.

Another respondent was more pragmatic about the necessity for the Society to 'manage' contentious issues, stating that:

> I suppose it would be the early years of the Troubles, it's probably documented somewhere a Meeting ... the question came up at Yearly Meeting and because of the theological and political diversity of Friends within the Yearly Meeting that wasn't, it hadn't been flagged beforehand and it wasn't the appropriate moment to get into detailed discussion, so it was suggested that there should be a meeting called for interested Friends and this took place in Churchtown [PM], and it was very interesting there that we got quite a broad spread of theological and political diversity there, having a session talking about the Troubles where we were coming from, the different angles.

Perhaps this sensitivity about openly discussing certain subjects also reflects norms in the wider society:

> Now you would always find out in Ireland, in the Republic, you would find out where people stood, what newspaper they read, what side their family was on, and then if it was the side, the awkward side, you just did not talk.

This sense of being silenced and silencing oneself was also experienced in other aspects of society:

> I suppose, I have probably silenced myself in a number of different situations. I would have gone to republican women's events and felt slightly uncomfortable there because I was an English Quaker. I would have gone to general women's events and probably felt things aren't being said here that I would like to be strong enough to bring up, and I would have been at

> Quaker gatherings and would have felt that certain issues relating to the conflict in the north of Ireland, were not appropriate to be raised either.

The previous quotations resonate somewhat with Rachel Muers' work which focuses on concerns expressed about a perceived lack of a common sense of English identity. Muers contends that an essential aspect of a shared identity is the silencing of certain groups of people or individuals because in order to preserve a distinctive identity, groups tend to exclude or silence those who do not 'fit' what is regarded as the template identity (2004, 111–112). It could be argued that 'silencing' then is not just about preserving unity but embedded in the Irish culture for the reasons given above. Muers suggests that:

> The theoretical aspects of this silencing includes the construction of the universal subject as (for example) male or European, and the exclusion of the concern of any other group from public consideration. (2004, 112)

Who the 'universal subject' is in the Irish Quaker context is complex and difficult to define. One respondent argued that IYM stays together because the alternative would be untenable:

> … the north-south divide is very deep in psychology even though there is a lot of reconciliation. The way we think, both actually, paradoxically unionists and nationalists in the north, I think are mentally in a very different place than in the south of Ireland. I think that that is probably quite a deep issue in Ireland Yearly Meeting because we are very happy to be together because if it wasn't it wouldn't be possible – we're so small. I think the strength of Ireland Yearly Meeting is we'll never split because it would be so frankly ridiculous, we're so small in numbers – we could not split in that way.

An example of organisational conflict which resulted in a schism occurred in Indiana Yearly Meeting in 2013, mainly due to tensions between liberal and conservative Friends over attitudes towards homosexuality (Stephen Angell, 2014). The next section explores this issue in the context of IYM.

4.10.2 Differing Interpretations of Quaker Theology

In recent years tensions within IYM have shifted from those related to Friends' political identity to theological and social aspects of identity. These identity categories are not separate entities but linked in complex ways. One of the issues consistently raised in the interviews was how the Society is responding to homosexuality and same-sex relationships. It appears that this has become a touchstone for some Friends about what it means to be an 'authentic' Quaker in the Irish context and reflects to a certain extent how some liberal and evangelical Friends differently interpret Quaker theology. One respondent expressed her shock at hearing a Northern Irish Friend referring to the Book of Leviticus in the Old Testament when the subject of homosexuality was being discussed and related this to her experience of having the scriptures mediated within Roman Catholicism:

> … is the first time that I got the 'shocker' of hearing Quakers talking like this. It was in connection with the new book [*Quaker Life and Practice*] that was coming out but it was away back in something like 2005 or 6 and I heard people from the north of Ireland condemning homosexuality on the basis of Leviticus, the passage in Leviticus. Now I mean to a Roman Catholic we have never used the Bible first-hand we've had it coming through the Church … I mean here's decades later, I thought I belonged to a terribly conservative Catholicism, decades later I'm here in … at this Meeting, and I hear this and I had left Catholicism because it was medieval and here I am back into the same thing again. I can understand condemning homosexuality if you feel unhappy about that kind of sexuality. I can understand that but I can't understand condemning it on the basis of scripture in the modern era that we're in – unless you're going to say I do not accept human investigation of an ancient document of scripture. If you say that then I also understand you but I say that's a very dangerous position to take. These are the things that we never totally ironed out.

These varying interpretations of Quaker theology were played out during the revision of *Quaker Life and Practice*. One respondent suggested that an awareness of the theological diversity of Friends was triggered by the revision process and this motivated Friends to attend the Yearly Meeting in greater numbers than usual:

> But that actually was an eye opener for a lot Friends because it was only when we started sending out the material to … and we sent it to each of the Preparative Meetings and the large Meetings around Yearly Meeting and feedback came back that some Friends suddenly discovered the theological diversity that there was within Yearly Meeting which they had not been aware of because people had been living in their own circle … Irish Friends had never as a Yearly Meeting discussed same-sex relationships so that was something that became a major issue towards

> the end. But I remember it was at one, one of the special Yearly Meetings and Ulster Friends had actually hired a bus and 35 people came down on a bus for the special Yearly Meeting, so this was wonderful that they were concerned and it included quite a few people from a particular Meeting which had normally only sent one or two Friends, so I knew that they were all there. I could see them and Friends from different parts of the country and Friends from the south as well, from around the Yearly Meeting.

Ross Chapman, a member of the Revision Committee,[50] described the sometimes tortuous process Friends went through attempting to find unity about the wording of contentious issues. In 2004 there were a series of events to commemorate 350 years of Quakerism in Ireland. During this year Friends were asked to consider an early draft of the new book. Chapman commented that 'And yet, unknown to the public, there was an immediate crisis at the heart of the Society' (2013, 19). Chapman went on to say that there were many objections to the proposed draft and that some Friends were not in favour of a new book. According to Chapman:

> They saw themselves as disciples of Jesus rather than disciples of the present age. Although aware of the changes within IYM, the evidence of this in cold print came as a shock. They felt betrayed. (2013, 20)

Conversely, some Friends felt that 'the draft had not gone far enough in representing a non-traditional religious perspective. They found the draft too prescriptive and needing more uncertainty as befits a questing religion' (2013, 20).

This section from *Quaker Life and Practice* about sexual orientation reflects how the different traditions of Irish Quakerism were eventually represented:

> Friends recognise that God has made us sexual beings. We unite in a desire to understand and value the spiritual insights of all our members and attenders regardless of their sexual orientation. We also however recognise that for some the physical expression of homosexuality is an occasion of spiritual struggle, confusion and profound distress. Some see it as a sin. We accept that more courage, prayer, knowledge and consideration are

50 A special committee of the Yearly Meeting called the Revision Committee was set up in 1999 to manage the process. Members were selected to reflect the theological and regional diversity of IYM (Chapman 2013, 17).

> needed as we seek to understand the mind of God and to love one another. (The Yearly Meeting of the Religious Society of Friends (Quakers) in Ireland 2012, 7.30)

Some respondents expressed great dissatisfaction with the final version of this section of *Quaker Life and Practice*. However, others mentioned that it helps that Irish Friends have various texts to choose from that match their theological perspectives, for example, liberal Quakers can draw on the British Quaker anthology *Quaker Faith and Practice* and are therefore not constrained by the Irish Quaker version. Some liberal Friends maintain close connections with BYM, drawing on opportunities to attend workshops and courses (personal correspondence, 2019).

The next section discusses how IYM seeks to maintain the unity of the organisation in the face of the diverse perspectives outlined earlier.

5 Management of Hybrid Identities by Ireland Yearly Meeting

As a response to the challenges of diversity within the Yearly Meeting, Irish Quakerism has developed a model of complex identity management which has been regarded by some Friends as leading to the avoidance of contentious subjects, but a necessary approach by others to keep together a small religious community and avoid a schism in the organisation. I argue that the relational unity of the Society was prioritised and that there was a conscious approach, when Friends were gathered together in regional or national Meetings, to find ways of 'managing' interactions between Friends to avoid 'harming' relationships when theological and political differences came to the fore. This section explores the different mechanisms employed to contain conflict in IYM and then goes on to identify the meaning of unity in the Irish Quaker context and how it was prioritised.

5.1 *The Structure of the Society*

In the previous section I outlined some of the cultural features of IYM and how these have evolved in recent years to emphasis the diverse identities contained within the Society. In this section I explore how the organisational structure of IYM enabled the management of this diversity.

I begin with a brief summary of the organisational structure of IYM shown in Figure 5. (Quakers in Ireland, structure). Starting from the bottom layer of the diagram are the 29 Preparative Meetings (PMs). Each PM has regular

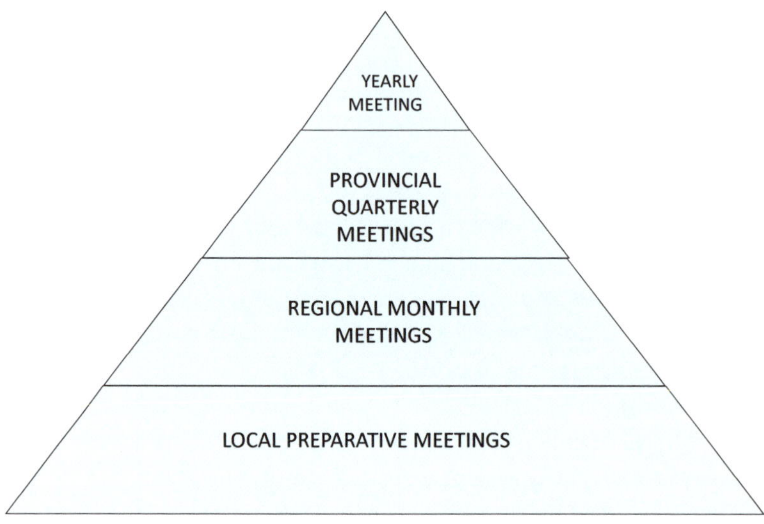

FIGURE 5 Organisational structure of Ireland Yearly Meeting

Meetings for Worship for business and sends representatives to the regional Monthly Meetings (MMs) which have the same function. The third layer of the structure of the Society is the Quarterly Meetings (QMs) which represent the provinces of Leinster, Ulster and Munster, and finally the Yearly Meeting. The locations of the Yearly Meetings rotate between different parts of the island of Ireland and in the past Friends have gathered in Dublin, Lisburn and Waterford. IYM met in Cork for the first time in 2013. The venue was significant and appeared to be linked to a wish to be inclusive of what is generally regarded by Friends as the most liberal part of the Yearly Meeting.

The pyramid shape of the diagram tends to convey the impression of a hierarchical organisational structure which does not fit the Quaker 'spirit-led' model of decision making. However, the Yearly Meeting has had to steer the Society through some very contentious decision making processes in recent years within a structure where there is considerable autonomy, particularly at the level of local PMs. This has inevitably meant that the Quaker business method has been adapted for the specific circumstances that operate in IYM to take into account the distinctive regional identities of Friends. For example, Chapman pointed to the particularly challenging circumstances around the revision of *Quaker Life and Practice,* referred to in section 4, stating that:

> All knew that the lofty ideals of Friends' business methods had not always been reached at our YMs and SYMs [special Yearly Meetings]. Over and over again, some or many Friends had felt aggrieved and not in unity

> with several of the recorded minutes. It seemed to them that majority rule was being practised. (2013, 26)

In addition, because the Yearly Meeting operates across both Irish states it has to encompass relevant legislation and social policy, and to respond to the financial implications of operating in two currencies. For example, one respondent talked about the difficulties of having different Child Protection legislation to contend with, which meant consistency of approach to this issue was problematic across IYM (field notes IYM, Dublin 2011).

Additionally, the decentralised structure of the Society encourages Friends to consider and test issues at each level before they go to the national body. The Quaker business method for making decisions is time consuming and some respondents found this way of doing things frustratingly slow. Harrison discusses modern Quaker belief in Ireland and is highly critical of what he regards as extreme liberalism and how it affects how Quaker business processes are understood. He refers to 'incomers' coming to Quakerism because they are unhappy about the authoritarian structures and creeds of their previous Christian denomination, but are not recognising Quakers have structures too, although they are very different from other Christian Churches (2006, 5). According to Harrison:

> A helpful recognition of 'diversity' has sometimes resulted in the suppression of any awareness that diversity should find its meaning in 'unity' and has been destructive of Quaker ideas of community. (2006, 6)

At the Yearly Meeting held in 2012 one of the sessions included feedback about a report of the Yearly Meeting Group on civil partnerships. This was in response to a letter received by the Yearly Meeting from Junior Yearly Meeting in 2010 following legislation on civil partnership that had been passed in the Republic of Ireland in 2004 and in Northern Ireland in 2005.[51] The report stated that 'the YM Nominations Committee was concerned that this group should not only represent the three QMs but also reflect the spectrum of opinion among Friends on this complex and challenging matter' (IYM 2012). In proposing to the Yearly Meeting that the decision about whether to have a special Meeting for Worship for civil partnership or not should be devolved to a local level, the authors of the report acknowledged the diversity of views among

51 The letter was from Young Friends expressing concern about the implications of the legislation on the Religious Society of Friends (Report of Civil Partnership Group to Ireland Yearly Meeting 2012).

members of the group and their lack of confidence that consensus could be found about this issue within the Society. It was further suggested that PMs were not obliged to agree to a request if it did not accord with the theological outlook of the Meeting, and if a Meeting for Worship was agreed upon, it would be a celebration of the civil partnership not a blessing. The clerk of the Yearly Meeting stressed that this was not a compromise. It was up to each PM to oversee these matters, asserting that 'they will be guided' and that there is already diversity about how funerals and other occasions are conducted (field notes, IYM, Dublin 2012)

I observed that the issue was managed very carefully: the report was read out verbatim and there was a short time allocated for Friends' reaction to the recommendations. My perception was that this was done deliberately to minimise potential for damaging conflict. One respondent talked about the way that Meetings for Worship for civil partnerships were dealt with – as an 'Irish solution to an Irish problem' – that is, half dealing with the issue but not fully dealing with it. This reaction contrasted with other respondents who also had a personal interest in the outcome. They suggested that it was progress which could not have been foreseen when the issue was originally raised. Interestingly the theme of that Yearly Meeting was 'Building Community', with the sub-heading, 'Dear Friends let us love one another, for love comes from God' (1 John Ch. 4 v 7) (field notes, IYM, Dublin 2012).

Although difficult the process of agreeing a position on civil partnership proved to be helpful for managing similar issues in the future, as one respondent observed:

> Last year IYM agreed to Marriage Equality, and in the Republic the first marriage has taken place. It is up to Monthly and Preparative Meetings to agree if they wish to do it, and no Quaker officiant is required to officiate in a marriage. If a Meeting cannot accept, they are to help the couple find a Meeting that will. The position of both views are recognised and respected. The divergence is not just a North/South issue. In Northern Ireland it is of course theoretical, because of the lack of legislation, but I reckon that at least half the Meetings would probably support same sex marriage. So we reached, relatively quickly this agreed position – partly because the experience of civil partnership had demonstrated that something like this was the only way forward. (personal correspondence, 2019)

The structure of the Society and how unity was promoted leads to another significant mechanism which is explored in the next section.

5.2 *The Role of Clerks and Other Key Individuals*

This comment by Rachel Bewley-Bateman, a former Yearly Meeting clerk, encapsulates my observations about the role of clerks in maintaining the unity of the Society:

> We have a broad theological spread and a very broad political spread and the … something which is always very important to us is the unity of the Yearly Meeting. We are sensitive to the diversity within our Yearly Meeting and endeavour to seek God's will for us all. Whether it is religion or politics, we are strengthened partly by family ties, and partly by denominational ties, if you want to call them that. The Yearly Meeting covers the 32 counties of Ireland and all clerks know that that is how we want it to be and how we want it to continue to be.

When contentious issues come to the Yearly Meeting they are very carefully 'managed' by the Friends responsible for the Yearly Meeting in session. According to a respondent, if a potentially divisive issue such as the revision of *Quaker Life and Practice* needed to be undertaken, there was careful structuring of how this would be managed, taking a long-term approach and waiting for certain Friends to carry things forward. This respondent said:

> … and it was waited on [until] we had a particular clerk … a lot of politics goes on in Quakers don't ever let anybody tell you there isn't. It is a very political organisation, it's small key but it's a political organisation … people if they want something to work okay they are very careful who they select to make it work … and there's a level of thought, long thought gone into something. There's a level of patience sometimes drives others up the walls even including myself about the urgency of doing things.

As indicated earlier in this publication, the 'Troubles' highlighted political divisions within the Society and made it difficult to bring this issue to the Yearly Meeting for open discussion. This extract from a contribution made by Friends to *The Believers Enquiry, 1997/98*, illustrates the way that the Society sought to preserve unity over this highly contentious issue:

> Something that we have all been very conscious of over the years is the importance that we have one united Yearly Meeting and that there shouldn't at any point, whether it be for religious or political reasons, be a division within the Society, and this has come before us in different

> times and different ways over the years ... Then equally at the early part of the Troubles, it was decided not to have a session at Yearly Meeting.... (Kenny 1998, 150)

This meant, for example, that the work of Quaker House would only be talked about in general terms rather than in specific ones. The other reason for circumspection about this 'Troubles'-related project was to do with the sensitivity of the work which involved confidential meetings between paramilitaries, politicians and others involved in conflict reduction dialogue.

However, this approach was not always effective, as a number of respondents observed, and is illustrated by Alan Quilley's observation that:

> We did become involved with a developing consciousness at one Yearly Meeting that there was a big rift between southern Friends and northern Friends, and there were some exchanges during the Yearly Meeting where it became quite clear that some of the southern Friends just had no idea what it was like to be living in the north. One was saying that she was surprised when she came north to see all these painted curb stones and this sort of thing. And so there was an attempt by the Yearly Meeting to set up regular meetings ... We were members of the peace process committee.

A number of respondents talked about the Yearly Meeting mentioned above, where things 'came to a head', and the response of IYM in setting up the peace process committee. One respondent observed that it was very significant that an evangelical Friend who had been personally affected by the 'Troubles' was on that committee. Friends generally appreciated the events that were organised to talk more openly with each other and share experiences of the 'Troubles', in order to improve communication between Friends in the Republic and Northern Ireland. Philip Jacob commented that:

> Our discussion was focused on emotions and identity. We tried to get a deeper knowledge and understanding of who we are, and how our backgrounds and experiences have shaped this view. (1996, 2)

At the end of one Yearly Meeting session, I observed that the reading included an extract from *Quaker Life and Practice* which emphasised unity and love. Felicity McCartney (the clerk of the Yearly Meeting at the time) said that there is a particular way in which things are talked about and that that is something that IYM really values. McCartney said that it is not possible to have these difficult conversations if Friends aren't willing to have these conversations in a particular way that involves openness but is very slow, saying that there has to be a slow approach; it has to be handled very sensitively with a great deal of respect for different views. McCartney added that Friends who threaten to withdraw or who become so committed to one particular perspective may not see or may not agree with this approach or are frustrated by it, which was apparent from my observations (field notes IYM, Dublin 2012).

5.3 *Countering Essentialism*

Another aspect of this complex identity management model is to tackle essentialisation within the Society. Essentialism refers to an understanding of identity which is based on the concept that it is formed by innate characteristics within people and is fixed, rather than shaped by social relationships and open to change.

According to Alvesson, this concept of identity can be over-simplistic when applied to organisations and needs 'careful interpretation' (2002, 187).

My findings suggest that IYM took conscious steps to help break down the boundaries between the different traditions within the Society. This was helped by the all-Ireland nature of the Religious Society of Friends and regular opportunities for Friends to meet one another. These include inreach events such as the one held in 2001 about exploring diversity within the Society.[52] Another example is the Yearly Meeting I attended in 2012 where there were activities that encompassed the different cultural and theological traditions such as hymn singing in Irish and English, a ceilidh (traditional Irish dancing and music) and a choice of either bible study or worship sharing at the beginning of the daily sessions. There were also the special interest groups such as RC to Q, referred to in the previous section.

A more inclusive approach was also evident at the local level of the Society, as illustrated by the following quotation:

> I went there and it happened to be the Sunday when they were reading the Query and they read it both in English and in Irish and I remember coming back to my own Meeting and saying just I was amazed in (name of PM) they have it in Irish as well … but sometime after that we started it in Irish in (respondent's PM) as well. They're small gestures I know

52 INREACH is work that builds communication and bonds between people within organisations. The INREACH event referred to above was the subject of an article in *The Friendly Word* (Archer 2001, 8–9) entitled INREACH 2001: Celebrating our Diversity which was a very positive account of the workshop.

> sometimes they seem to be artificial and superficial and external. To me they aren't – they speak volumes about an openness.

The use of the Irish language during Meetings for Worship appeared to have a very positive impact on the respondent who is from a culturally-Catholic background. Friends from Meetings in the Republic and Northern Ireland were also encouraged to visit each other (Jacob 1996, 2). A respondent talked about how her understanding of Friends in Northern Ireland had changed since getting to know them:

> I got to know Friends in the north so much better from staying with them and how I have got quite close to some of them even though, now we're all kisses and hugs when we meet and people at my Meeting [ask] what's going on there?… What we did we went round to each other's Quarterly Meetings and stayed with one another and I got to know how things were on the ground in a lot. I stayed with an attender in (name of PM) Meeting whose son was attending Friend's school Lisburn and in his local Protestant community he was getting beaten up because they said 'you're not a real Prod. Quakers are not real Prods.'

The example above tends to support the 'contact hypothesis' outlined in Mitchell and Ganiel's work, which suggests that when people who have very different, potentially 'oppositional', identities meet and get to know each other they tend to moderate their views and become more open-minded (2011, 116). The next section explores what unity represents in the Irish Quaker context.

5.4 *The Meaning of Unity for Irish Friends*

My findings suggest that for Irish Quakerism conflict management and ways of promoting unity are intrinsically linked. As was outlined previously, conflict was managed through the structure of the Society, for example, by devolving certain contentious decisions to the local level. The role of individual Friends, particularly clerks of the Yearly Meeting, was significant and time was taken to wait for the appropriate conditions when difficult issues were to be addressed. Care was taken to nominate Friends from the different traditions within the Society when a committee was established, such as the support committee for Quaker House and the Yearly Meeting group on civil partnerships, so that their recommendations had the required authority.

The principles of unity and love (prioritising relationships) were stressed in national gatherings, especially when Friends were 'discerning' the way forward in their decision-making. It was very important to Friends that the all-Ireland nature of the Society was maintained. This meant at times that certain issues (particularly related to the 'Troubles') were not taken to the Yearly Meeting but were discussed separately. There was also a conscious approach to reflect the diversity of the Yearly Meeting in the content of Quaker events and there were inreach activities to enable Friends to learn about each other's perspectives. However, Friends recognised that there is a limit to how much these approaches can overcome some of the fundamental differences between them. This respondent's comment appears to encapsulate what unity means in the Irish Quaker context:

> There's a big difference between unity and uniformity. Let's do what we can together but have the freedom to do things in our own particular way.

Thus it can be argued that the factors outlined above indicate that Irish Friends have developed a form of relational unity which is dependent on strengthening bonds between each other while leaving major differences intact. The risks inherent in the maintenance of unity through Friends' relationships will now be discussed.

5.5 *Friends' Responses to Identity Management*

This section considers some of the challenges that Irish Quakerism faces to maintain the unity that has been achieved so far. It can be argued that unity based on relationships can be harder to maintain and more difficult than unity based on doctrine or ideology. Relational unity relies more heavily on the Quaker business method and discernment, the roles of key individuals and events that encourage social bonding. In addition, it can be contended that IYM has a strong corporate identity in the sense that it encompasses a wide range of diversity in its membership. However, that doctrinal unity in the Society is weaker because of this diversity. When unity is sought to make progress on contentious issues brought to the Yearly Meeting, the differences between Friends' views and backgrounds are highlighted and this can undermine their sense of relational unity. For example, it could be argued that the decision to devolve decisions about Meeting for Worship for civil partnerships to the PMs weakens national unity; building in a mechanism which accentuates regional and theological differences creates a form of inequality at a local level, although the Yearly Meeting stays together. Unity is also likely to be more difficult to maintain in PMs which have a greater mix of identities than those that are mainly liberal or evangelical in tone.

There is already some splintering occurring at the local level as some Preparative Meetings become semi-detached from the national organisation.

Some respondents commented that a large evangelical PM is becoming more congregational, for example, with the publication of doctrinal statements on their website about homosexuality and civil partnerships. A liberal PM in the same QM also publicised their very different position on the same issue. The different positions about this ongoing social issue seems to raise questions about how a clear message about what Irish Quakerism stands for is formulated by the Society.

Friends responded in different ways to how IYM managed the tensions resulting from the complex identity of individuals within the Society. For example, some Friends bypassed the practice of testing concerns at different levels of the Society, which in any case had been adapted to avoid bringing certain 'Troubles'-related matters to the Yearly Meeting. An example is Victor Bewley, whose role as an intermediary was referred to in section 4. According to his daughter, Rachel Bewley-Bateman, if Victor Bewley had followed the usual procedure for testing his concern it would have exposed the strong feelings of some Friends that contact with 'the men of violence' was not in accord with the peace testimony, and would have delayed his response to requests to help facilitate communication between members of the IRA and the British Government. Bewley therefore acted on a more individual basis with the support of local Friends and not on behalf of Quakers nationally.

Some respondents recognised that a schism in the Yearly Meeting has been avoided, but observed that this has been at some cost and there were Friends who were critical of the lack of 'positioning' (Quaker 'neutrality') of IYM during the 'Troubles'. Other respondents expressed the view that there was a possible 'sectarian' bias evident in how the peace testimony was interpreted on occasions, referring to the 'lack of unity' about an application for membership from an attender who was a member of Sinn Féin. This is an example of something that several respondents mentioned with regard to feeling 'silenced' by the convention in the Society at that time of not highlighting political divisions.

5.6 *Quakerism as a Meta-identity*

This section considers whether there is evidence to suggest that the identity category 'Quaker' helps with unity because it rises above other identity labels and creates space from 'worldly' identities that remind Friends of their differences. As one Friend wrote in the article, 'Establishing Quakerism in the Irish Culture': 'even if we do come from different cultures, if we can listen to the holy Spirit, communication is possible across the divide' (Crowley 1997, 9). This Friend also stresses the importance of seeing Quakerism as a worldwide organisation that can overcome national and political boundaries (Crowley 1997, 9). However, my findings show that some respondents did not share this perspective about the international context of the Religious Society of Friends and their national identity was very important to them.

It can be argued that for liberal Yearly Meetings such as BYM, Quaker as a meta-identity works reasonably well because there is a general acceptance that, as Dandelion argues, in liberal theology belief is marginal and what is prioritised is the 'behavioural creed'; worship based on silence allows for differences to be masked or contained. However, in IYM there isn't one over-arching identity that Friends subscribe to. Within the Society there are many identities including evangelical and liberal traditions and different national identities. Consequently, it is less clear what the shared identity is for Irish Quakers and there is no 'universal subject', a concept outlined by Rachel Muers.

In my research I found many examples of bridge-building by individuals and by the corporate organisation to overcome differences between Friends and to develop a stronger Quaker meta-identity. For example, in drawing up the Report of Civil Partnership Group for IYM, the committee used a form of language that consciously emphasises the values that Friends share by identifying a list of core values underpinning Quaker beliefs regarding same-sex attraction (Ireland Yearly Meeting 2012). These values include: acceptance and mutual respect, a non-judgemental attitude, commitment to social justice and equality, and welcoming and supporting the spiritual development of all people drawn to Quakerism irrespective of their sexual orientation.

However, there is clearly disagreement about how these values should be carried out in practice, particularly between those Friends who focus on the testimonies and others who are more biblically-based. Liberal Friends also put different emphasis on which of the testimonies they feel most drawn to and have varying interpretations of what they mean; for example, the Friend who used the language of the testimonies of truth and equality as part of his 'coming out' journey within Quakerism. There were also other Friends during the 'Troubles' who understood that the peace testimony necessarily involved dialogue with republican and loyalists paramilitaries, despite the disapproval of some Friends who had a different understanding of the same testimony.

Therefore, it is possible to argue that Quaker as a meta-identity for Friends in Ireland is both strong and weak depending on the circumstances. It can work when differences between Friends are de-emphasised and common values are highlighted. It is more problematic when Friends individualise their Quaker identity and attachment to different and possibly conflicting ways of being Quaker. It is also noteworthy that respondents had different degrees of connection to their Quaker identity and for some it was one of a number of equally significant identity categories. However, there is some evidence that

Quaker as a meta-identity works better on a political level for some Friends as a way of challenging sectarianism in the wider society.

6 Conclusion

In this publication I argued that sectarianism has had a distinctive impact on the Religious Society of Friends from the organisation's early settlement in Ireland. The violent conflict in the country was a challenge to Friends' peace testimony. Friends' response was to avoid taking sides in sectarian-related conflict. The 'Troubles' in Northern Ireland brought the issue of political neutrality to the fore again when the hybrid and diverse identity of IYM was highlighted by the sectarian basis of the conflict.

Within the Religious Society of Friends in Ireland societal, political and regional factors create distinctive local Quaker cultures. For example, a significant theological divergence occurred within the Society triggered by the mid-nineteenth century evangelical revival which had a strong influence on Ulster Friends. After the partition of the country in the 1920s the divergent social and political dimensions of the newly created Irish Free State and Northern Ireland had a further impact on the regional culture of Quakerism. As Friends adjusted to the new political systems, they continued to maintain their all-Ireland structure and ethos which was facilitated by the Quaker family dynasties. However, a political divergence was beginning to open up in the Society as some Friends became more actively involved in the structures of the new Irish states.

The publication discusses observations by some of the Friends interviewed namely that the culture of Irish Quakerism has undergone further changes for a number of reasons, including the impact of Friends from culturally-Catholic backgrounds, who tend to be one of the main sources of Friends joining by 'convincement' and liberal in their theological outlook. Some respondents raised concerns about how newcomers to Quakerism learn about how things are done, for example, in terms of the Quaker business method. This point illustrates the different perceptions of 'birthright' and 'convinced' Friends – the latter sometimes wanting to change Quaker processes because they regard them as too slow and not responsive enough to current events. Conversely, some 'birthright' Friends expressed concern that Quaker tradition and culture will become too 'diluted' because of the influence of Friends from different cultural and theological backgrounds (particularly Catholicism).

The Quaker identity matrix illustrated the diverse and hybrid identity of individual Friends. For example, I found that Friends from Catholic backgrounds in the Republic of Ireland tend to remain culturally-Catholic despite taking on an identity as a member of a nonconformist denomination. In terms of their national identity, these Friends have what Todd refers to as a 'banal' or taken for granted identity as members of the majority group in the Republic. The perception that Quakerism is a mainly Protestant, British middle-class institution has caused them some discomfort. Some Friends from other Christian backgrounds gave examples of Catholic 'sectarianism' and portrayed a sense of having to try harder to be accepted as fully Irish, although according to some of my respondents this appears to be changing. This last finding chimes with Todd's work about the 'symbolic distinctions' that operate in both of the Irish states, which create a sense of belonging or exclusion.

It can also be argued that these distinctions were also visible within IYM, but played out differently than in the wider society. 'Symbolic distinctions' within Quakerism were not directly Catholic and Protestant (although these were in the background) but more to do with tensions between Friends about the 'true' nature of Quakerism. There was clear evidence from the interviews that a different relationship to being Quaker was demonstrated by some Friends, in particular over claims that Quaker theology is about the testimonies (by liberal Friends) or about traditional Christian beliefs (by evangelical Friends). Liberal Friends also used a broader range of terms when they described their spiritual life than evangelical Friends, and some were also exploring other spiritual or humanistic paths. Some evangelical Friends observed that the theological direction of the Society seemed to be moving away from its Christian roots and a belief in biblical truths and salvation towards a greater emphasis on social activism.

All of the respondents avoided self-identifying as Protestant for a number of reasons. For culturally-Catholic Friends there are negative associations attached to joining a Christian denomination identified with religious and political divisions. Other Friends do not regard themselves as 'culturally' Protestant and those using the labels 'Quaker not Protestant' (or in some instances Dissenter) see these labels as offering a third way through sectarian divisions in the wider society, especially in Northern Ireland. However, many of the respondents were aware of Quakers, especially in the rural areas of Northern Ireland, who more closely reflect the Protestant unionist profile of some communities there, although I was unable to interview anyone from this strand of Irish Quakerism to confirm this for myself.

The evidence about identity negotiation and transcendence was outlined mainly in the case studies in section 4. There is the example of 'Peter', a Northern Ireland Friend, who challenged sectarianism in his community and workplace. His choice of party political affiliation and dual national identity demonstrate his commitment to finding a middle way through sectarianism. He also acted as a 'bridge' between the different theological strands of Irish Quakerism. The other example is of 'Sean', whose hybrid identity encompasses different strands of potentially 'oppositional' labels, that is, someone from a nationalist background and culturally Catholic in a minority nonconformist denomination in the Republic of Ireland. He demonstrates a capacity to critically examine 'sectarian' aspects of his cultural heritage and find ways of relating to other Friends from very different political and theological backgrounds. There was also evidence of other Friends who had a pivotal role in bridge building within the Society, especially in terms of the liberal/evangelical division. The significant role of certain Friends, particularly 'birthright' Quakers from the evangelical wing of IYM, in helping to make progress on contentious issues was something that was raised by many respondents. These Friends acted as cross-over figures between the different traditions within the Society.

During the 'Troubles', a number of Friends were actively involved in cross-community projects that sought to challenge sectarianism and reduce sectarian-related violence. Some Friends were also members of non-Quaker groups and organisations with similar aims. Quaker Service is a registered charity in Northern Ireland that maintains a commitment to this work.

IYM manages tension and conflict about contentious issues which result from the diverse perspectives and backgrounds of its membership; other faith groups are struggling with similar issues, such as attitudes towards homosexuality and the role of women in the Church. As Steph Lawler posits:

> If ... people have multiple identities and identification, does every group belonging rely either on the suppression of some forms of identity or an endless internecine strife between different factions within the category? (2014, 167)

I argued that one of the consistent themes from the interview data was that the unity of the Society was viewed as being paramount and that when Friends talked about what they meant by unity they referred to the avoidance of harming relationships or hurting each other's feelings by highlighting political and theological differences. I termed this form of unity 'relational' as opposed to other types centred on doctrine or ideology. Other Friends found this approach problematic and felt that conflict had been silenced and that on occasions they had silenced themselves, and wanted more openness and discussion about areas of disagreement. I also outlined the ways in which relational unity was maintained in IYM. This was done through the structure of the organisation, by Friends in key roles, by using the Quaker business method in a particular way when contentious decisions were made, and by organising events that encompass the different traditions and give Friends opportunities to develop closer connections. At the same time there is recognition that differences in how Friends relate to their Quakerism remain intact but that in order to avoid harming relationships it is necessary to consider how these are expressed. As one respondent remarked:

> The paragraph quoted for many years on the front of *The Friend* 'in essentials unity in non-essentials liberty in all things charity'… for Quakers is important.

Another respondent recognised the positive aspects of bringing contentious issues out into the open in a sensitive way. He said:

> Although painful the subject of homosexuality has helped people talk about things, which is actually quite healthy. Previous to this there was never any need to discuss things like this, everything was done by instinct. You were aware of things you said and things you did not say. You were aware of what the other people thought because you'd grown up with them all your life, so you did not really have to have some huge discussion about [these issues].

Douglas Kline argues that the meaning attached to conflict generally within the Society of Friends has changed over time in that:

> Conflict was once central to the Quaker cultural model, as Friends sought to bring a new millennium through a 'lamb's war'. When Friends established the peace testimony, 'conflict' was no longer central to their engagement with the world for the Quaker interpretation of the world. Today, unity dominates the Quaker imagination particularly in the process of decision-making as Friends form minutes, which reflect the general will of the decision-making body. Quakerly dispositions enact particular strategies and tactics in the management of conflict situations. Withdrawal and avoidance are typically recognised as the primary means to manage conflicts within the Society, using silence and self-questioning to forestall overt dispute. Yielding is common when Friends aim to lay aside their needs for the sake of the social contract or the wider body. In these situations the relationship is viewed as more important than the personal need. (2002, 320–321)

Kline contends that it was relational not doctrinal unity that was prioritised in BYM, which has parallels with my findings about Irish Friends. Like Kline, Susan Robson explores the issue of conflict in BYM and contends that Friends are more comfortable focusing on conflict in the wider world than on internal conflict (2008, 142). Robson is overtly critical of what she regards as conflict avoidance within the organisation, as the following quotation illustrates:

> This study shows the obverse of the espoused theory that Quakers should mend the world and live in a peaceable kingdom without conflict. It shows that Quakers avert their minds from their own conflicts, which do exist. When this proves impossible they are uncertain and unskilled in handling them. This is the position from which they encourage the rest of the world to resolve its conflicts. (2005, 231)

Robson asserts that her study uncovered many examples of conflict within BYM and that Quakers are no different from other groups in this respect. She found that the two main responses to conflict were aversion and prioritising community relationships over finding the 'right' outcome for the conflict (2008, 143–144).

Robson and Kline's observations about BYM chimes with my findings about relational unity being so important for Quakers in Ireland. It is interesting to note that unlike Irish Quakerism, theological differences were not identified as a major source of conflict by the British Friends interviewed for Robson's study (2008, 147). Robson goes on to suggest that the culture of Quakerism, as it operates in Britain, restricted the development of positive ways of handling internal conflict and that in order to make progress on conflict management in the future it would be necessary for Friends to examine some of the fundamental values within their cultural identity (2005, 232).

Robson also contrasts how conflict is managed by British and Irish Quakerism and highlights what she considers is the inadequate approach of BYM compared to IYM (2008, 155). She asserts that the two Yearly Meetings mirror the culture of the societies where they are located in terms of approaches to conflict, and that Quakerism in Britain 'reflects the polite and restrained tradition of not talking about religion or politics' (2008, 155). Robson goes on to suggest that:

> … in a tradition riven by religious affiliation enacted in politics Ireland Yearly Meeting is robust enough to grasp the nettle of conflict with firmness. (2008, 155)

The implication that Irish Quakers are much more open about their differences and tackle conflict robustly and that this is the norm in Ireland, contrasts somewhat with the observations of my respondents. Robson's observations seem to be largely based on impressions gained from limited information about conflict-management in IYM and give a rather narrow impression of the situation.[53] My findings indicate that how conflict is managed in Ireland is much more complex.

Irish Quakerism faces a number of challenges to maintain the unity that has been achieved so far. It can be argued that unity based on relationships can be harder to maintain and more difficult than unity based on doctrine or ideology. Relational unity relies more heavily on the Quaker business method and discernment, the roles of key individuals and events that encourage social bonding. In addition, it can be contended that IYM has a strong corporate identity in the sense that it encompasses a wide range of diversity in its membership. However, that doctrinal unity in the Society is weaker because of this diversity. When unity is sought to make progress on contentious issues brought to the Yearly Meeting, the differences between Friends' views and backgrounds are highlighted and this can undermine their sense of relational unity. For example, it could be argued that the decision to devolve decisions about Meeting for Worship for civil partnerships to the Preparative Meetings weakens national unity, building in a mechanism which accentuates regional and theological differences and creates a form of inequality at a local level, although the Yearly Meeting stays together. Unity is also likely to be more difficult to maintain in Preparative Meetings which have a greater mix of identities than those that are mainly liberal or evangelical in tone.

Finally, I found that 'Quaker' has the potential to work as a meta-identity, particularly on an external, political level but that it was more problematic within the organisation. This is demonstrated by how some Friends have consciously developed a Quaker identity that is neither Catholic nor Protestant to sidestep negative sectarian connotations. This stance was validated when the planning of the Quaker House project was in its early stages. Members of other Christian denominations perceived that Friends were ideally placed to take the work forward, as this quotation illustrates:

> … one of the reasons behind the evolution of Quaker House was the fact that at the time in the '70s, late '70s, when this was being thought about,

53 In her most recent work Susan Robson revised her observations about conflict handling in IYM and acknowledges the difficulties there were in managing certain contentious issues within the Society (2014, 70).

> there was definite encouragement from the other Churches to do this because they felt Quakers were in a place in the middle. They weren't perceived as either Protestant or Catholic and therefore they were the people who could actually be in this position and do something in this sort of political area.

The label 'Quaker' was claimed by these Friends as being a third way – encompassing their own potentially 'oppositional' identity categories. This means that perceptions of Quaker neutrality and their anti-sectarian stance gave Friends involved in 'Troubles'-related work a strong basis in terms of establishing credibility and trustworthiness with the nationalist and unionist communities during the conflict. It can be argued that by modelling an alternative, non-sectarian identity, Friends are building capacity with other individuals and organisations with a similar ethos, for identity transformation in both of the Irish states.

Acknowledgements

This monograph is based on my doctoral thesis and I thank Ben Pink Dandelion, my supervisor, and the other academic staff and students at the Centre for Research in Quaker Studies, Woodbrooke. I am very grateful to Friends in Ireland for their hospitality; for sharing their insights and knowledge of Irish Quakerism, and for being willing to participate in my research study.

References

Alvesson, Mats. 2002. *Understanding Organizational Culture*. London: SAGE Publications.

Anderson, Gerry. 2000. "The Routes of English." Radio 4, broadcasted 30 November 2000. http://www.bbc.co.uk/radio4/routesofenglish/storysofar/programme3_2.shtml. Accessed 24 May 2010.

Angell, Stephen. 2014. "Separation Accomplished: New Beginnings for a New Association of Friends and a 'Reconfigured' Indiana Yearly Meeting." *Quaker Theology* 24, no. 13: 1.

Archer, Gerda. 2001. "INREACH 2001: Celebrating our Diversity." *The Friendly Word* 18, no. 6: 8–9.

Bayar, Murat. 2009. "Reconsidering Primordialism: An Alternative Approach to the Study of Ethnicity." *Ethnic and Racial Studies* 32, no. 9: 1639–1657.

Bennett, Ann. 2009. "Quaker House Belfast." In *Coming from the Silence: Quaker Peacebuilding Initiatives in Northern Ireland 1969–2007*, edited by Ann Le Mare and Felicity McCartney, 91–121. York: William Sessions Limited.

Berresford Ellis, Peter. 2004. *Eyewitness to Irish History*. Hoboken, NJ: John Wiley & Sons.

Bloomfield, Kenneth. 2007. *A Tragedy of Errors: The Government and Misgovernment of Northern Ireland*. Liverpool: Liverpool University Press.

Book of Christian Discipline of the Religious Society of Friends in Ireland. 1971. The Yearly Meeting of the Religious Society of Friends (Quakers) in Ireland. Waterford: Friendly Press.

Bruce, Steve. 2009. *Paisley: Religion and Politics in Northern Ireland*. 2nd ed. Oxford: Oxford University Press.

Burdsey, Daniel, and Robert Chappell. 2003. "Soldiers, Sashes and Shamrocks: Football and Social Identity in Scotland and Northern Ireland." *Sociology of Sport Online* 6, no. 1: 1–23. http://www.pyshed.otago.ac.nz/sosol/v6i1/v6i1.html. Accessed 7 June 2011.

Butler, Judith. 2011. "Big Think" video series. Transcript of a video recorded 13 January 2011. http://www.bigthink.com/videos/your-behavior-creates-your-gender. Accessed 16 March 2015.

Cantor, Geoffrey. 2001. "Quaker Responses to Darwin." *Osiris* 16: *Science in Theistic Contexts*, 321–342.

Chapman, Arthur. 2009. "Some Initiatives of Friends." In *Coming from the Silence: Quaker Peacebuilding Initiatives in Northern Ireland 1969–2007*, edited by Ann Le Mare and Felicity McCartney, 16–32. York: William Sessions Limited.

Chapman, Ross. 2013. "Irish Quakers Create a New Book." *The Friends Quarterly* 41, no. 1: 16–28.

Clayton, Pamela. 1998. "Religion, Ethnicity and Colonialism as Explanations of the Northern Ireland Conflict." In *Rethinking Northern Ireland: Culture, Ideology and Colonialism*, edited by David Miller, 40–54. London and New York: Longman.

Cochrane, Feargal, 1997. "The Unionists of Ulster: An Ideological Analysis." Centre for the Study of Conflict, University of Ulster. http://cain.ulst.ac.uk/issues/politics/union/fcchap2.htm. Accessed 5 March 2012.

Coleman, Simon, and Peter Collins. 2004. Introduction: "Ambiguous Attachments: Religion, Identity and Nation in Religion." In *Identity and Change: Perspectives on Global Transformations*, edited by Simon Coleman and Peter Collins, 1–25. Aldershot: Ashgate.

Collins, Peter. 2008. "The Problem of Quaker Identity." In *The* Quaker *Condition: the Sociology of a Liberal Religion*, edited by Pink Dandelion and Peter Collins, 38–52. Newcastle: Cambridge Scholars Publishing.

Coogan, Tim Pat. 1995. *The Troubles, Ireland's Ordeal 1966–1995 and the Search for Peace*. London: Hutchinson.

Coohill, Joseph. 2008. *Ireland: A Short History*. 3rd ed. Oxford: Oneworld Publications.

Crowley, Ita. 1997. "Establishing Quakerism in the Irish Culture." *The Friendly Word* 14, nos. 1–2: 9.

Daly, Mary. 2007. "The Irish Free State/Éire/Republic of Ireland/Ireland: A Country by Any Other Name?" *Journal of British Studies* 46, no. 1: 72–90.

Dandelion, Pink. 1996. *A Sociological Analysis of the Theology of Quakers: The Silent Revolution.* Lampeter: The Edwin Mellen Press.

Dandelion, Pink. 2008a. "The Creation of Coherence: The Quaker Double-Culture, and the Absolute Perhaps." *In The Quaker Condition: The Sociology of a Liberal Religion*, edited by Pink Dandelion and Peter Collins, 22–37. Newcastle: Cambridge Scholars Publishing.

Dandelion, Pink. 2008b. *The Quakers: A Very Short Introduction.* Oxford: Oxford University Press.

Darby, John. 1995. "Conflict in Northern Ireland: A Background Essay." Centre for the Study of Conflict, University of Ulster. http://cain.ulst.ac.uk/othelem/facets/htm. Accessed 21 June 2010.

Douglas, Glynn. 1998. *Friends and 1798: Quaker Witness to Non-Violence in 18th Century Ireland.* Dublin: Historical Committee of the Religious Society of Friends in Ireland.

Douglas, John. 2004 [1954]. *The Beginnings of Quakerism in 17th Century Ireland.* An address given at the Quaker Tercentenary Conference in Friends School Lisburn July 1954. *Occasional Papers in Irish Quaker History*, no. 2. Dublin: Historical Committee of the Religious Society of Friends in Ireland.

Duke, Elizabeth. 2012a. "It Makes All the Difference: Does Salvation Have Meaning for Friends?" *The Woodbrooke Journal* 29: 1–25.

Duke, Elizabeth. 2012b. "Listening to Quakers in Ireland. Part of a study of Friends' understanding of salvation. Unpublished field notes.

Egenolf, Susan. 2009. "Our Fellow-Creatures: Women Narrating Political Violence in the 1798 Irish Rebellion." *Eighteenth-Century Studies* 42, no. 2: 217–234.

Elliott, Marianne. 2009. *When God Took Sides: Religion and Identity in Ireland – Unfinished History.* Oxford: Oxford University Press.

Equality Commission for Northern Ireland: ECNI. http://www.equalityni.org/Footer-Links/Legislation. Accessed 7 March 2012.

Farrell, Seamus. 2009. "Quaker Peace Education Project." In *Coming from the Silence: Quaker Peacebuilding Initiatives in Northern Ireland 1969–2007*, edited by Ann Le Mare and Felicity McCartney, 121–145. York: William Sessions Limited.

Fitzduff, Mari, and Liam O'Hagan. 2009. *The Northern Ireland Troubles.* INCORE background paper. Centre for the Study of Conflict, University of Ulster. http://www.cain.ulst.ac.uk/othelem/incorepaper09.pdf. Accessed 17 May 2010.

Foster, Roy, ed. 1992. "Ascendancy and Union." In *The Oxford History of Ireland*, 134–173. Oxford: Oxford University Press.

Frayling, Nicholas. 1996. *Pardon and Peace: A Reflection on the Making of Peace in Ireland.* London: SPCK.

Ganiel, Gladys. 2016. "A Charismatic Church in Post-Catholic Ireland: Negotiating Diversity in Abundant Life in Limerick City." *Irish Journal of Sociology* 24, no. 3: 293–314.

Ganiel, Gladys, and Paul Dixon. 2008. Religion, Pragmatic Fundamentalism and the Transformation of the Northern Ireland Conflict. *Journal of Peace Research* 45, no. 3: 419–436.

Goodbody, Robin. 1995. *Quaker Relief Work in Ireland's Great Hunger, 1846–1849*. Kendal: Quaker Tapestry Booklets.

Goodbody, Robin. 1998. "Quakers and the Famine." *History Ireland* 6, no. 1: 27–32.

Grange Friends Meeting. http://www.grangefriendsmeeting.co.uk. Statement of Belief. Accessed 30 July 2013.

Greaves, Richard. 1997. *God's Other Children: Protestant Nonconformists and the Emergence of Denominational Churches in Ireland, 1660–1700*. Stanford, CA: Stanford University Press.

Guiton, Gerard. 2005. *The Growth and Development of Quaker Testimony 1652–1661 and 1960–1994: Conflict, Non-Violence, and Conciliation*. Lampeter: The Edwin Mellen Press.

Hall, Stuart. 1996. Introduction: "Who Needs Identity?" In *Questions of Cultural Identity,* edited by Stuart Hall and Paul du Gay, 1–17. London: SAGE Publications.

Hancock, Thomas. 1844. *The Principles of Peace, Exemplified in the Conduct of the Society of Friends in Ireland, During the Rebellion of the Year 1798: with some Preliminary and Concluding Observations*. London: Charles Gilpin.

Harrison, Richard. 2006. *Merchants, Mystics and Philanthropists: 350 Years of Cork Quakers*. Cork: Cork Monthly Meeting.

Harrison, Richard. 2008. *A Biographical Directory of Irish Quakers*. 2nd ed. Dublin: Four Courts Press.

Hatton, Helen. 1993. *The Largest Amount of Good: Quaker Relief in Ireland 1654–1921.* Montreal: McGill-Queen's University Press.

Hennessey, Thomas. 2005. *Northern Ireland: The Origins of the Troubles*. Dublin: Gill & Macmillan.

Inglis, Tom. 2007. "Catholic Identity in Contemporary Ireland: Belief and Belonging to Tradition." *Journal of Contemporary Religion* 22, no. 2: 205–220.

Jacob, Philip. 1996. "Conference Report." *The Friendly Word* 13, no. 2: 2.

Jenkins, Richard. 2000. "The Limits of Identity: Ethnicity, Conflict, and Politics." *Sheffield Online Papers in Social Research* 2. http://www.sheffield.ac.uk/polopoly_fs/1.71447!/file/2jenkins.pdf. Accessed 19 August 2014.

Jenkins, Richard. 2014. *Social Identity*. 4th ed. Abingdon: Routledge.

Kennedy, Maria. 2016. "The Religious Society of Friends (Quakers) in Ireland: Sectarianism and Identity." Unpublished PhD thesis. University of Birmingham.

Kenny, Colum, ed. 1998. *"Imprisoned Within Structures"? The Role of Believing Communities in Building Peace in Ireland (The Believers Enquiry)*. Glencree, Glencree Centre for Reconciliation.

Kline, Douglas. 2002. "Quakerly Conflict: The Cultural Logic of Conflict in the Religious Society of Friends." Unpublished PhD thesis. University of Edinburgh.

Lampen, John. 2011. *Answering the Violence: Encounters with Perpetrators*. Pendle Hill Pamphlet 412. Wallingford, PA: Pendle Hill Publications.

Lawler, Steph. 2014. *Identity: Sociological Perspectives*. 2nd ed. Cambridge: Polity Press.

Liechty, Joseph, and Cecelia Clegg. 2001. *Moving Beyond Sectarianism: Religion, Conflict, and Reconciliation in Northern Ireland*. Dublin: The Columba Press.

Lockhart, Audrey. 1988. "The Quakers and Emigration from Ireland to the North American Colonies." *Quaker History* 77, no. 2: 67–92.

Macallister, Peter. 2011. "From Catholicism to Quakerism." *The Friendly Word* 28, no. 6: 12.

McCartney, Clem, ed. 1999. "Introduction." In *Striking a Balance: The Northern Ireland Peace Process. Accord* 8, 10–18. http://www.c-r.org/accord/northern-ireland. Accessed 17 March 2011.

McCartney, Felicity. 2009. "Introduction." In *Coming from the Silence: Quaker Peacebuilding Initiatives in Northern Ireland 1969–2007*, edited by Ann Le Mare and Felicity McCartney, 1–15. York: William Sessions Limited.

McKittrick, David, and David McVea. 2001. *Making Sense of The Troubles*. London: Penguin Books.

McNicholl, Kevin. 2019, "The Northern Irish Identity: Attitudes Towards Moderate Political Parties and Outgroup Leaders." *Irish Political Studies* 34 (1): 25–47.

Melaugh, Martin, and Brendan Lynn. 2005. *A Glossary of Terms Related to the Conflict*. Centre for the Study of Conflict, University of Ulster. http://www.cain.ulst.ac.uk/othelem/glossary.htm. Accessed 12 May 2010.

Miller, David. 1998. "Colonialism and Academic Representations of the Troubles." In *Rethinking Northern Ireland: Culture, Ideology and Colonialism*, edited by David Miller, 3–39. London and New York: Longman.

Minihan, Julianna. 2011. "RC to Q: Coming to Quakerism from Roman Catholicism." *The Friendly Word* 26, no. 4: 4–6.

Mitchell, Claire. 2006. *Religion, Identity and Politics in Northern Ireland: Boundaries of Belonging and Belief*. Aldershot: Ashgate.

Mitchell, Claire, and Gladys Ganiel. 2011. *Evangelical Journeys: Choice and Change in a Northern Irish Religious Subculture*. Dublin: University College Dublin Press.

Moloney, Ed. 2007. *A Secret History of the IRA*. London: Penguin Books.

Mowlam, Marjorie. 2002. *Momentum: The Struggle for Peace, Politics and the People.* London: Hodder and Stoughton.

Muers, Rachel. 2004. "New Voices, New Hopes?" In *Towards Tragedy/Reclaiming Hope: Literature, Theology and Sociology in Conversation*, edited by Pink Dandelion, Douglas Gwyn, Rachel Muers, Brian Phillips, and Richard Sturm, 108–123. Aldershot: Ashgate.

Neill, Joyce. 1999. *Denis Barritt Cheerful Saint.* Kelso, Scotland: Curlew Productions.

O'Connor, Ulick. 1989. *The Troubles: The Struggle for Irish Freedom 1912–1922*. London: Mandarin.

Ó hEithir, Breandán. 1989. *A Pocket History of Ireland.* Dublin: The O'Brien Press.

Parker, Martin. 2000. *Organisational Culture and Identity: Unity and Division at Work.* London: SAGE Publications.

Pollak, Andy, ed. 1993. *A Citizens' Inquiry: The Opsahl Report on Northern Ireland.* Dublin: The Lilliput Press Ltd.

Punshon, John. 1984. *Portrait in Grey: A Short History of the Quakers.* London: Quaker Home Service.

Quaker Faith and Practice: The Book of Christian Discipline of the Religious Society of Friends (Quakers) in Britain, 2013. 5th ed. London: The Yearly Meeting of the Religious Society of Friends (Quakers) in Britain.

Quaker Life and Practice: A Book of the Christian Experience of the Religious Society of Friends in Ireland, 2012. Dublin: The Yearly Meeting of the Religious Society of Friends (Quakers) in Ireland.

Quakers in Britain. http://www.quaker.org.uk/more-about-testimonies. Accessed 25 September 2010.

Quakers in Ireland. http://quakers-in-ireland.ie/about-us/structure/. Accessed 7 November 2014.

Reay, Barry. 1980. "Quaker Opposition to Tithes 1652–1660." *Past & Present* 86, no. 1: 98–120.

Report of Civil Partnership Group to Ireland Yearly Meeting 2012. Unpublished report.

Robson, Susan. 2005. "An Exploration of Conflict Handling Among Quakers." Unpublished PhD thesis. University of Huddersfield.

Robson, Susan. 2008. "Grasping the Nettle: Conflict and the Quaker Condition." In *The* Quaker *Condition: the Sociology of a Liberal Religion*, edited by Pink Dandelion and Peter Collins, 140–157. Newcastle: Cambridge Scholars Publishing.

Robson, Susan. 2014. *Living with Conflict: A Challenge to a Peace Church.* Plymouth: Scarecrow Press.

Rynne, Colin. 2008. "The Rolt Memorial Lecture 2007 Technological Change as a 'Colonial' Discourse: The Society of Friends in 19th-Century Ireland." *Industrial Archaeology Review* 30: 1.

Shils, Edward. 1957. "Primordial, Personal, Sacred and Civil Ties: Some Particular Observations on the Relationships of Sociological Research and Theory." *The British Journal of Sociology* 8, no. 2: 130–145.

Sinton, Joan, and Billy Sinton. 1984. "The Light from Number 7." *The Friendly Word* 1, no. 2: 4.

South Belfast Quakers. http://www.southbelfastquakers.org/sbq/Beliefs.html. What we Believe. Accessed 14 October 2014.

Stroope, Samuel. 2011. "How Culture Shapes Community: Bible Belief, Theological Unity, and a Sense of Belonging in Religious Congregations." *The Sociological Quarterly* 52, no. 4: 568–592.

Todd, Jennifer. 2005. "Social Transformation, Collective Categories and Identity Change." *Theory and Society* 34, no. 4: 429–463.

Todd, Jennifer. March 2010. "Symbolic Complexity and Political Division: The Changing Role of Religion in Northern Ireland." *Ethnopolitics* 9, no. 1: 85–102.

Todd, Jennifer. 2012. "Social Structure and Religious Division: Comparing the Form of Religious Distinction in the Two Irish States." Paper presented at the *Religious Conflict and Difference Conference*, Stranmillis University College, Belfast.

Todd, Jennifer, Theresa O'Keefe, Nathalie Rougier, and Lorenzo Cañás Bottos. 2006. "Fluid or Frozen? Choice and Change in Ethno-national Identification in Contemporary Northern Ireland." *Nationalism and Ethnic Politics* 12, nos. 3–4: 323–346.

Toolis, Kevin. 1995. *Rebel Hearts: Journeys within the IRA's Soul*. London: Picador.

Tosh, John and Seán Lang. 2006. *The Pursuit of History: Aims, Methods and New Directions in the Study of Modern History*. 4th ed. London and New York: Longman.

Tweed, Thomas. 2006. *Crossing and Dwelling: A Theory of Religion*. Cambridge, MA: Harvard University Press.

Vann, Richard, and David Eversley. 1992. *Friends in Life and Death: The British and Irish Quakers in the Demographic Transition 1650–1900*. Cambridge: Cambridge University Press.

Wigham, Maurice. 1992. *The Irish Quakers: A Short History of the Religious Society in Friends in Ireland*. Dublin: Historical Committee of the Religious Society of Friends in Ireland.

Yearly Meeting of Friends in Ireland Statistics 2010. Internal paper. Ireland Yearly Meeting 2011.